For Alex,

Sorry, more weeds than
Wisdom for Californians !

Hatsy T.

WEEDS AND WISDOM

FROM A COUNTRY GARDENER

BY
HATSY TAYLOR

Landloper Press

Library of Congress Catalog Card Number 00-107168

ISBN # 0-9703362-0-9

FOR HANK

who did all the heavy work -

rototilling the garden, mending

the fences, mulching the asparagus,

but above all else,

keeping this gardener happy for 45 years

ACKNOWLEDGEMENTS

Thank you, Robin, for being not only a great editor but a great friend. Thanks as well to all the other friends who gave their help – Turi, Louise Angie and Kirk

I would also like to thank the various newspapers in which the columns in this book first appeared: The Lakeville Journal, The Berkshire Eagle and The Register Citizen of Torrington.

And of course many thanks to Mother Nature for providing inspiration.

Printing by Rainbow Press, Torrington, Connecticut 06790

CONTENTS

INTRODUCTION

I was born with a love of the land, but my career as a gardener didn't begin until 1962 when my husband and I bought Locust Hill, a 250-acre farm at the end of a dead-end road. The farmhouse, sloughing off its nubbly gray stucco as if it were suffering from some hideous skin disease, had been abandoned for six years, its only occupants a dozen dead starlings dumb enough to come down the chimney and a rabble of lively rats.

We didn't care. Having escaped the commuters and cocktail parties of Fairfield County, we were as happy as a rabbit that's found a bolt hole from a hungry fox. We'd come back to the land. Beyond the farmhouse lay acres of open meadow, woodland and a vista view of Canaan Mountain to the south.

Having bought the farm in January, we had no idea what lurked beneath the winter's snowy covering. A pristine white blanket of snow can hide a disreputable landscape as deceptively as smooth talk and slick promises can disguise a crooked politician. It was only when April's warm sun laid bare the horrors of the yard that I realized it was time to become a gardener.

Every corner of the yard cried out for help. The area in front of the house bristled with burdocks, their burrs delighting in the opportunity to snag a ride on passing dogs, cats and children. Less hazardous, but more unsightly than these pernicious weeds, was the overgrown half-dead hedge of hemlocks that cut off all that beautiful winter sunlight from the front of the house.

Aged, decrepit lilacs, as sad looking as an unemployment line during the Depression, scratched plaintively at the windows on the western side of the house. Beyond these mildewed bushes the land sloped down to a swampy morass of reeds and saw grass that had once been a cow pasture.

The backyard was equally charming - a falling-down woodshed decorated in ropes of poison ivy, a collapsing cement retaining wall and a healthy stand of nettles. In fact, the entire area surrounding the house could have been declared a disaster area. I was not much of a gardener, but it was fairly obvious that I should hurry up and become one.

Fortunately the area requiring renovation was limited. The acres of smooth green meadows and hilly pastures, eventually dotted with sheep, that lay beyond the yard in every direction had not been abandoned and needed no improvement. Even so, it took many years before Locust Hill became presentable.

Lawns, flower beds, a vegetable garden, asparagus and raspberry beds - through trial and error - I learned the ins and outs and do's and don'ts of good gardening. Because all the house repairs were a top priority - wiring as frayed and frazzled as a salesgirl at Macy's on Christmas Eve, pathetic plumbing and a wood burning furnace that smoked us out into the yard the first and only time we used it — they took what little money we had, leaving mere pennies for the new gardener.

As a result I became an expert on acquiring something for nothing. I scoured our hilltop's woods and fields for freebies from Mother Nature - dogwood trees, laurel, bittersweet. I learned to beg, barter and upon occasion even steal (if you call snitching myrtle growing wild behind the cemetery or pocketing seed heads from the public garden stealing) in order to transform Locust Hill's junkyard appearance into an attractive landscape.

During those years I was a full-time mother of three, traveled around the country giving wildflower programs to garden clubs to augment our finances and worked alongside my husband in his manufacturing business, but the garden projects were what kept me sane. Financial difficulties, marital difficulties, daughter difficulties – what got me through life's trials was my love of the farm.

Over the years I collected so many gardening experiences that I began writing a weekly column for the local newspapers called "Weeds and Wisdom." After a few months I attempted to illustrate some of the columns, and despite the fact that I was dubbed Grandma Moses the 2nd by the two daughters who are now professional artists, I kept at it, even taking one or two art courses along the way.

It's been close to twenty years since I began writing and illustrating Weeds and Wisdom and I'm still at it. Since garden ideas rarely become outdated, choosing which columns to put between the covers of a book has been great fun as I relived the years of turning Locust Hill into a respectable, well-groomed property.

I had no problem melding two or three columns into one, cutting or adding to others, but arranging them by subject matter or by season seemed to take away their flavor, so I left them alone. Please use the Index to find specific subjects.

I've never considered myself a horticulturist, just an entertainer, so you'll no doubt glean more weeds than wisdom from these tales. Raspberries, radishes, lupines and llamas - they cover every aspect of life on Locust Hill. Hopefully you'll find them entertaining, but also harvest a few good tips on raising vegetables and flowers, trees, shrubs and even daughters.

THE VEGETABLE GARDEN

I was brought up in an era when the vegetable garden had yet to come out of the closet. It was considered to be on a par with the clothesline, the propane tank and the doghouse, an eyesore to be hidden from view. Such utilitarian items as sprawling tomato plants and bolting lettuces were not expected to mar the clipped lawns and landscaped areas near the house.

Even though most of these niceties were still in the distant future, I followed in the footsteps of my mother and grandmother, putting the garden way up behind the heifer barn. It was a major mistake. Considering the amount of work that goes into a vegetable garden, choosing a poor site is like stumbling at the starting line - the race is lost before you've begun.

The site I picked had plenty of sun, the most important ingredient for a successful garden. Good soil, the next necessity, it definitely did not have. Locust Hill's soil is basically gray clay more fit for a potter's wheel than growing plants, and stones enough to sink a dozen murdered Mafia victims. Good soil, however, can be created with the addition of compost and manure and a lot of work.

It was the site's other drawbacks that couldn't be cured. I learned very quickly that I couldn't hear the telephone or keep an eye on the children when I was picking beans or killing potato bugs. With the first dry spell I realized that getting water to the garden meant carrying buckets. Worst of all, I discovered that deer, woodchucks and rabbits all thought my vegetables had been planted just for them.

Ah, but the garden was out of sight where it should be. Of course "out of sight" tends to mean "out of mind," so more often than not my faraway garden contained a host of overripe, unharvested vegetables, smothered in pigweed and purslane. Conversely, when I did go up to tackle the

1

weeds or water a row of thirsty lettuce, I would forget everything else. I don't know how many times I put eggs on the stove to boil and then left them to turn into popping fire and brimstone while I was happily staking tomato plants or mulching the broccoli.

It took ten years of burned eggs, missed phone calls and neglected produce before I faced the fact that the garden should be close to the house. By then the backyard had been converted into a respectable lawn. Once it became the new vegetable garden, I couldn't imagine why I'd ever hidden the original garden up behind the barn. The colors, textures and shapes of vegetables offer as much variety as those of flowers, and serve double duty – good to eat as well as pretty to look at.

Having the garden only a few steps from the kitchen door had dozens of advantages. Besides deterring marauding wildlife, it eliminated the watering problem and the necessity of mowing a back lawn. The sudden need for a scallion for the salad or parsley for the lamb chops was no longer a chore. Neither was a quick trip to the compost pile.

The most thrilling advantage was how sheltered the new site was from late and early frosts. The garden up behind the barn was totally unprotected, sitting in lonely splendor in the big meadow. It once suffered a visit from Jack Frost in mid-June, another year on the 15th of August. Try producing a juicy red tomato under those conditions!

The one flaw in having a garden close to the house is the one Mother and Grandmother worried about. It can become an eyesore if it's neglected. The chores of weeding, staking and harvesting, being only a few steps away from the bed-making and the bill-paying, are easier to get to, but if you neglect them you may find your backyard resembling a city slum by summer's end.

FLOWERS FOR DESSERT

Basic landscaping - creating lawns, planting shrubs and trees, making a vegetable garden - these are the meat and potatoes of gardening, but what sort of gardener wants to go through the summer without a piece of pie? Flowers are the gardener's dessert, be they in a window box, a hanging basket or a perennial bed. Such delicious choices - the white fluff of Candytuft, tiny clumps of crocuses, sweet-smelling carnations, rich spires of delphiniums, all as tempting as the selections displayed on a dessert cart at Schraft's.

Unfortunately I was on such a strict diet in the first years I gardened on Locust Hill (soon to be renamed Low Cost Hill by the children) that I had little time for such delicacies. A packet of flower seeds is cheap, however, so I always devoted at least one row of the vegetable garden to annuals. And planting a collection of mixed annuals, my choice as a beginner, provided me with a rudimentary education in many of the flowers I was unfamiliar with.

Although my pocketbook could handle a few packets of seeds, I never attempted to start any perennials. That was probably a good thing since I was still a complete neophyte in the art of gardening. I knew so little about perennials I assumed from their name they'd bloom all summer and live forever without help from the gardener.

I had no idea that many perennials need to be divided every four or five years, that division results in multiplication, and this results in excess plants. My friend Bunny, loathe to dump such extras on the compost pile, started me down the perennial path with a bucket full of iris rhizomes. Irises were never my favorite flowers, but I'm not one to refuse a freebie. I accepted the weird looking roots, got directions on how to plant them and looked around for an appropriate place to put them.

3

In front of the split rail fence that divided the new lawn from the sheep pasture seemed like a good spot. They looked pretty silly there all alone, but that summer I acquired a new friend whose flower garden was overflowing with old-fashioned blooms - daisy-like feverfew, shaggy-headed beebalms, stately clumps of phlox. All I did was admire this garden to have Jeannette start digging up plants.

I spaced these new treasures between my clumps of iris. Next it was my mother, dividing her lemon lilies. Then my friend Marty moved out of state and insisted I take the lupines and peonies she was forced to leave behind. Pretty soon, by dividing and multiplying all these gifts, my border of "hand-me-downs" had crept more than half the length of the fence.

A flower garden that "just growed" like Topsy may sound like a crazy idea, but it is a wonderful way for a beginner to learn about plants without spending a lot of money. The slick advertising and glossy photographs in garden catalogs rarely inform readers of a plant's flaws.

I soon realized that sheep like phlox blossoms enough to climb their fence to reach them. I discovered that evening primrose isn't a primrose at all, that its little rosettes of leaves can turn into dozens of rosettes in a single year. I learned through painful experience that lupine stems can turn gray and fuzzy overnight as swarms of aphids gather to suck their lifeblood.

But the most important aspect of a perennial bed that I learned about was when each of my plants would come into flower, something that can vary considerably from place to place. Plants that live in the northwest corner of Connecticut, known locally as "The Icebox," bloom two or sometimes even three weeks later than those living in warmer climates. Keeping a record of these dates allowed me to eventually have continuous bloom in the border throughout the season.

THE AGONY AND ECSTACY OF ASPARAGUS

The Taylor tale of asparagus woes includes so many errors that I'm an expert on what NOT to do to have a successful crop. To begin with, DON'T plant your roots in the wrong place. That was our first mistake. When you realize your asparagus bed is right where you want the swimming pool or the carport or the swing set, moving those roots to a better spot doesn't work. When we tried it, carefully transplanting ours into a deep new trench, we had no idea we were attending a funeral, but that's what it was. Not one plant survived the move.

Being a penny pincher, I decided to buy seeds instead of roots for my next attempt. DON'T. Unless you're the sort of patient person willing to start with baby chicks to get laying hens, I don't recommend this method of starting an asparagus bed. Seeds are very slow to germinate and must be grown in individual containers as they transplant poorly.

Buying one or two-year-old roots is by far the best way to start a bed. And buying roots through a catalog is a safer bet than hoping you'll find them at the local nursery. That was another one of my mistakes, discovering too late that there were no roots to be had at the local nurseries.

The old-fashioned way to prepare an asparagus bed fortunately went out of style along with chores like beating rugs and darning socks. One no longer has to dig a three-foot deep trench, one foot will do. Fill the bottom with rich compost and well-rotted manure until it is only 6 inches deep.

Asparagus roots look like baby octopuses with arthritis. Spread out their stiff legs in a circle and cover them with loose dirt, leaving just their heads showing. Tamp the dirt firmly and water thoroughly. It's important not to let the roots dry out during the next few weeks. Soon the first green shoots appear. As they grow, fill in the trench around them until it is full, then mulch.

No picking. Not that you'll be tempted. The stalks are as thin and tasteless as plastic straws. In the fall you can cut down the stalks, or leave them to die a natural death, in which case you'll be able to tell where the following year's new stalks will appear. During a snowy winter mice and moles like to make a maze of tunnels under the mulch, but they seem to do no harm.

In the spring remove the mulch from part of the bed so the soil can warm up, providing you with early shoots. Let the rest come up through the mulch. If weeds get in the bed, you can spread coarse salt on the area. Asparagus likes salt and weeds do not.

What is more delicious, fresh asparagus with hollandaise, cold marinated asparagus with fresh lettuce or creamed asparagus on toast? Ever tried dipping cooked asparagus in the fondue pot? It took us close to ten years to worry about such things as too much asparagus, but eventually we did get a bit tired of having this gourmet vegetable for dinner four or five nights in a row each June, along with filling the freezer with the excess.

The solution to that problem is a tricky one, but it works. Try harvesting stalks from only half the bed in the spring and letting the other half turn into a forest of feathery stalks. In late August, cut down the stalks in the second half of the bed. They will quickly produce fresh tender asparagus.

The only problem with this idea is that there are too many delicious fruits and vegetables ripening at the end of summer – corn, tomatoes, melons. Who needs asparagus? The best time to try this second crop is when you've taken a vacation in June and been unable to harvest the spring crop. Just remember, the ground is hot in August compared to June, so spears appear in a matter of hours instead of days.

THE GREENSWARD

A mowed lawn is one of the few improvements man has been able to make in Mother Nature's landscape. Her prairies and mountain meadows may look smooth and beautiful from a distance, as do pastures that have been grazed, but try walking through them in your bare feet. No, there's no real substitute for the incredibly green velvet of Spring's grass carpet, the deep blue-green of a maple-shaded summer lawn, or the pristine white blanket that stretches in unbroken splendor after a winter snow.

When I was growing up in West Hartford, one of our more fancy neighbors replaced the front lawn of his estate with a private six-hole golf course. A few years later, World War II's gas rationing forced him to let it turn into a field. We kids played infinitely more delightful games than golf in that luxuriant meadow, matting down secret tunnels and serpentine paths that led to sweet-smelling nests on the overgrown putting greens.

Most country clubs kept their golf courses mowed during the war by using their members' pooled gas coupons, but one club found a better way. They fenced the course and grazed sheep on it. Each ewe was outfitted with a football helmet to protect her from flying golfballs!

In 1972 when the Arabs got nasty, environmentalists urged us to turn our lawns into meadows full of wildflowers. That idea may sound appealing, and it would certainly eliminate the weekly chore of mowing, but much as I love wildflowers, I wouldn't call it an adequate substitute for the greensward.

We have lots of lawns on Locust Hill. For years I mowed them with a push mower. Then one daughter after another grew old enough to do the job. Eventually they all left home and I took over again until my back went out and I had to hire a yard kid. Hank does not do lawns.

The problem with yard kids is that they always seem to mow so the grass clippings are dumped into the borders. There is hardly a single lawn edge on Locust Hill that can tolerate having grass thrown at it. The ivy-covered stone walls look terrible with clumps of old dead grass clinging to them, the myrtle and pachysandra beds would be a mess in no time, and of course the flower beds would soon produce an astronomical weed problem.

Fed up with the latest incompetent kid, Hank and I sat down one night and figured out the cost of hiring another (I'd fired the last one) vs. buying a riding mower. Providing we amortized the cost over five years, we found the mower would make economic sense. Even so, I didn't like the idea. In my opinion, riding mowers are suburban toys bought by overweight executives so they can cut their postage-stamp lawns without losing any of those excess pounds.

There was also a major problem – trying to get around all the tricky little corners and banks and dead-end areas on the property that required a hand mower. Since most of them were even hard to do with a hand mower, it made good sense to try and eliminate them, so Hank made a diagram and marked each trouble spot with an X.

The worst one was a 6'x10' patch of grass beside the propane tank. On its right is the animal barn, on the left the top of a retaining wall and at the back the fake outhouse we'd built to hide the propane tank. Obviously this small lawn should be replaced with pachysandra and maybe a couple of flagstones so the gas man could read the meter through the half-moon window of the outhouse.

There were other X's that no sane person on a riding mower would tackle, plus lots of square corners that needed to be turned into curves. By the time we identified them all, my back ached just thinking about all the work it would take to fix them. Somehow, with the help of a new yard kid, we managed it, and that fall (when riding mowers went on sale) we bought a second-hand one for $500.

We thought it would last five years but with pampering, it kept going for ten. By that time riding mowers had so many built-in safety features we could hardly believe it. America seems to be set on eliminating risk. What ever happened to the pioneer spirit that built this country??!!!

Being a mere five feet tall, I found the first two safety features almost impossible. The mower wouldn't start unless the clutch was pushed down so far that with my short legs I had to lift my weight off the seat, which automatically stalled the motor. How's that for a Catch-22? Hank solved this problem by putting a block on the pedal.

On top of these two exasperating precautions, the mower had a large cover sticking out on the side to prevent idiots from putting a hand too close to the whirling blade. This cover, however, also prevented the machine from mowing sideways on the slightest slope. When we removed it, the grass clippings spewed out at least eight feet.

One more safeguard it took me a while to remember was the fact that the cutting blade stopped automatically whenever I went into reverse. After backing up for some difficult spot of the yard, I would uselessly chug ahead again for several minutes without cutting any grass.

Oh well, eventually I learned to live with all these new features, and now I am as happy as a fat suburban CEO, tooling around the lawns each week.

POND PROBLEMS

When we bought our 250-acre farm back in 1962 it didn't have a pond. What it did have was a brook that turned into a swamp just below the house. Hank and I envisioned turning this area into a pond, using the removed dirt to level the area above it for a lawn and burying a pipe under the lawn to carry the brook's water to the pond.

When we had finally gotten the farmhouse habitable and began landscaping the yard it was August. The little brook had turned into a mere trickle, but our dream hadn't changed. In fact we'd already asked the County Agricultural Agent for advice on where to build the pond. Unfortunately his recommendation was not what we wanted to hear.

"You'll have nothin' but problems, you put it in that hollow," he warned. "That's the old road bed used to go to Massachusetts. Soil's too sandy, and prob'bly full of rocks." Looking around the yard, he pointed to the area above our planned lawn where we'd envisioned a sheep pasture. "Best put your pond up there. Good clay soil, and plenty of seepage."

It's a smart idea to heed the advice offered by an expert in the field, but putting the pond above our planned lawn would mean we'd be unable to see anything but its dam. We wanted to enjoy the sight of blue sky reflected in blue water, watch barn swallows dip and skim, hear the bullfrogs chuggarum at dusk. We decided to ignore the agent's recommendation.

As a consequence, the pond leaked more seriously than a congressional committee listening to secret testimony. We ended up paying for our stubbornness. During the excavation the bulldozer encountered one car-sized rock that couldn't be moved. The water level went up and down like the tide. Each spring and fall the pond was brimming and beautiful, but by June, as the brook slowed to a sick trickle, the water level slipped until the dinosaur rock reared its ugly head and was revealed in all its craggy glory.

Our frustration was at least partially removed, however, the year we spent a weekend with friends who'd built a sauna in their back yard. We came home inspired. Our farm neighbor George had just replaced his old silo with a new one, and was happy to let us take the old tongue-and-groove silo staves. We built a round Hottentot house at the end of the lawn, put in a kerosene stove, a platform and four slingback canvas chairs and had ourselves a sauna.

Suddenly our useless pond became swimmable in April and May, October and November. Its icy water felt delicious after fifteen minutes in our 200-degree Hottentot house. Taking a dip after a sauna on Thanksgiving weekend became commonplace, at least for daughters and sons-in-law, if not for us old folks.

The other problem we had with the pond was a common one, weeds. Like most mud-bottomed ponds, ours became mired in weeds every summer. In the early years, before we became environmentally conscious, we killed the weeds with copper sulfate. It did the job, but then someone told us about a fish being raised in Arkansas that ate weeds.

The weed eaters were a species of carp called white amurs that are found in the Amur River in China. For many years they were banned from most New England states as exotics. Now I'll be the first to agree that undesirable wildlife should be banned from our state. I'm glad we've outlawed such things as the Kudzu vine that spreads faster than measles at a birthday party and is equally unpleasant. I wish we could outlaw the gypsy moth and the Japanese beetle. But putting the amur on a list of illegals is like putting a banana peel on a list of lethal weapons.

Amurs can lay up to one million eggs at a time. That sounds pretty threatening if you have a mama and a papa in your quarter-acre pond, unless you understand the conditions required to hatch those eggs – water that flows at least eight feet per second, is between 68 and 74 degrees, and has a pH level between 7.0 and 7.4. That's just for starters. Even if those conditions are met, the eggs won't hatch unless they're constantly moving for at least 36 hours.

All these essentials are being artificially created in Arkansas where amurs are raised commercially, but even in those controlled conditions, the fish won't breed unless pumped full of hormones. We ordered a dozen, not knowing they were illegal. The fish farm happily took our order, neglecting to mention the Connecticut ban.

We met the fish at the airport and rushed them home to a huge repast of pond weeds. In two years they had gobbled up all the greenery in sight and had doubled in size. The next summer I began feeding them grass clippings each Friday after I mowed the lawn. They splashed so eagerly for this treat that we started giving them corn husks whenever we had corn for dinner.

The amurs find any vegetable matter edible. They even try to eat the apples that fall into the pond from the apple tree, but rarely succeed. They are uninterested in frog eggs, tadpoles or even the tiny goldfish from the Five and Ten Cent store that eventually grew bigger than a lupine blossom.

They are very timid. We never see them when we swim. Maybe a swimmer with long green hair might tempt an amur to attack, but I doubt it. The barn swallows love zeroing in on the shadowy fleet like fighter planes, scaring them into diving to the mud bottom in a swirl of white water.

Having grown up with a mud-bottomed pond, I don't mind swimming with a few fish and frogs. What I don't like are bloodsuckers, and I'm happy to report, we don't have any of these disgusting creatures.

ORCHARD FAILURES

My parents planted a 12-tree orchard just a few years before I was born, so I grew up along with plums, pears, peaches and three kinds of apples. No part of my childhood was happier than the hours I spent balanced on a leafy limb, contemplating life and enjoying the super crunch of a green apple, or the juicy warm sweetness of a sun-ripened plum. Naturally I wanted our kids to have these same pleasures, but it wasn't until some friends moving out of the state had a tag sale that included "dig your own dwarf fruit tree for a dollar" that we began our orchard.

That summer - 1965 - was as dry as a fly that's died in a hot air register. New trees need water in their first year more than anything else, but carrying buckets that far...well, we've never been super good at maintenance. Only the peach tree survived. It produced an amazing crop of peaches though, and it was such a treat to have free fruit that we scraped together enough money to put in a Granny Smith apple and a Green Gage plum.

The mini orchard was located next to the remains of the collapsed cow barn, and the year it began producing, the local farmer who cut our hayfields offered to bulldoze and level the barn foundation, at the same time increasing the size of the field. Since he didn't want the orchard in his enlarged meadow, he lifted each fruit tree with his back hoe and replanted it along the fence of the lower sheep pasture just below the pond. None survived the move.

It was almost five years before we considered another attempt. We chose dwarf trees, knowing that regular fruit trees would eventually block our view of Canaan Mountain. If you've never had the joy of clambering from limb to limb in a large cherry tree, resting among the leaves and blue sky at the top of the world, all secret and unseen except by the bees and birds who share the heady perfume and fruit, you might be excused for planting dwarf trees, but I should have known better.

Yes, they're easier to spray (if you bother to spray) and make harvesting easier, and never grow tall enough to block the view, but they aren't good for climbing, or even strong-limbed enough for a kid's swing. We might still be living with those midgets if a freak rainstorm in September 1977 hadn't dumped five inches of water into our pond, washing away the dam. Our little brook turned into a raging torrent that cut a 20-foot gully right down the fence line. Next morning we found a small piece of our rowboat down on Route 44, but we never did find our dwarf fruit trees.

By then I was more than a half-century old and no longer as eager to spend my days clambering from limb to limb. Nor did I have the same desire for tart green apples I'd had as a child with a cast iron stomach. No more attempts were made to have an orchard.

A NOT SO SECRET GARDEN

When we first moved to Locust Hill there was a small stone building in the backyard with its backside dug into the slope of the pasture. A hired man had built it around the turn of the century, preferring to sleep in this dank, windowless hovel than in the house. Someone had later added a cement floor, making the ceiling so low you couldn't stand up inside. We used the building for storing garden tools, broken furniture, tricycles and trash. It became known as the Alotta because it housed such alotta junk.

One evening as we were eating dinner, we heard a loud crash, followed by the frantic bellowing of a cow. When we rushed out the back door, we discovered one of our neighbor's heifers inside the stone hut, thrashing around in the midst of rotted roof beams and alotta junk. Since the building's roof was on a level with the pasture at its back edge, this silly young cow had lumbered onto it and fallen through. She was too big to get out through the door, so we spent the next hour pulling down most of the front stone wall in order to free her.

As we began hauling away the debris the next day, it suddenly occurred to me that what remained of the Alotta could be turned into a garden. Not quite The Secret Garden in Francis Burnett's book I'd found so appealing as a kid, but at least a semi-secret one, a space 8 feet by 10, bounded on three sides by the remaining stone walls of the hut.

The first step in creating the garden was to remove the cement floor. Hank got the pickax and began breaking it up into pieces small enough to be lifted, while I hitched the trailer to Venerable, the tractor we'd inherited with the farm. Unfortunately a monstrous amount of stone had been used below the floor so this first step took two days.

We filled the resulting hole with dirt and well-rotted manure and rebuilt the front wall into a foot-high edging for the garden. By that time it was too late to do much planting, but I stuffed the ripe seeds of wild columbine between the cracks of the back wall and transplanted a little English ivy that would hopefully climb up it.

For the next ten years - no, to be honest, ever since - I've experimented with my walled garden, trying to get it just right. I may have wanted to turn this semi-secret spot into a deliciously appealing garden, but I sure didn't know how to go about it. My first approach, since the vegetable garden was still up behind the barn, was to plant a tiny kitchen garden - tidy rows of lettuce, radishes, carrots.

That idea lasted only as long as the path of old bricks I'd laid out between the rows. Dandelions and other determined weeds eagerly settled between the bricks, their roots turning the red clay into shards. Jack Frost did his share of damage as well, until my once handsome paths looked like a Roman ruin.

I replaced them with stepping stones leading to a sunken birdbath in a corner of the back wall (now decorated with ivy), planted white phlox behind it and a mixture of perennials and annuals on either side of the path. Every few years I'd try something new, rip out something that didn't seem to fit. My first real success was a variety of miniature daffodil called Tete-a-tete. When these tiny yellow trumpets bloomed on their four-inch stems around the edge of the pool, they looked perfect and made me realize that big plants belong in alotta garden, smalls in abitta one.

I renamed the Alotta the Abitta, but it never stuck. I did, however, stick with the small plants, putting white thyme as a ground cover among the Tete-a-tetes, baby's breath as a background for a variety of the smaller annuals, from pansies to petunias. The Alotta garden still isn't quite what I pictured, but it's given me alotta fun.

AUTUMN LEAVES

When you live with something all your life, it's easy to take it for granted - Mother Nature's autumn extravaganza, for instance. I'm not saying we don't revel in the amazing colors each fall when our deciduous trees blaze with red and gold, but how many of us stop to think how lucky we are to be able to enjoy this palette of pigments? New England is one of the few places in the world where it occurs.

Most folks think Jack Frost starts our colorful display, cutting off the production of chlorophyll that hides other leaf pigments. T'aint true. A layer of cells called the abscission layer at the base of the petiole of each leaf cuts off photosynthesis by producing an enzyme that digests the cell walls. This is a programmed response built into the life cycle of deciduous trees to prepare them for winter when there is insufficient water to counteract leaf evaporation.

Once the strong green pigments in each leaf have stopped working, the yellow pigments, carotene and xanthophyll, are revealed, along with the scarlet and purple pigments called anthocyanins. All these colorful tints require high light intensities and high sugar content for their development.

When the show is over, we gardeners face the chore of raking up all those leaves. We had so few trees on the farm when we moved here that we didn't need to rake. Farmers rarely plant trees. More often than not, they cut them down to give their crops more sunlight. Besides the indigenous locust trees that grew in the fence lines on the hill, and the acres of woodland beyond the meadows, we had a sugar maple whose trunk was no bigger around than a gallon jug and whose leaves were conveniently swept down the hill by the north wind; an ancient apple tree and a weeping willow with a hollow heart that blew down our first winter.

Over the years, the trees that we planted got bigger and bigger, but it wasn't until 1992 that we had so many autumn leaves that the north wind couldn't handle the job. Having always bragged about not having to rake leaves, we finally got our comeuppance. Much to our horror, we discovered that the leaves we'd not bothered to rake the previous fall were still there, wet soggy piles of them killing the grass everywhere we looked. It became very obvious that Locust Hill's "No Rake" yard had vanished forever.

Leaf raking causes blisters, back aches and bursitis. Furthermore we no longer have the reward of lighting a match to the pile and reveling in that pungent smoky perfume. Like rumble seats and running boards, the mystery of sandwiches wrapped in waxed paper on a picnic and the fun of rolling butterballs between serrated wooden paddles for Thanksgiving, the fragrance of burning leaves is a thing of the past.

The ban on leaf burning makes sense, but it's a shame that the lovely smell wafting, blue and hazy into the crisp autumn air, had to also be banned. I bet someone could make a fortune bottling the essence of burning leaves.

Since we can no longer indulge in leaf burning, we might as well put all those leaves to work. Pachysandra loves a blanket of oak or maple leaves during the winter. So do laurels, azaleas and evergreens. Less acidic leaves such as ash, apple, poplar or locust rarely need raking as they decompose quickly if not raked into a pile. And of course it doesn't take long for a pile of leaves in the compost bin to turn into something as dark and rich as chocolate cake.

WHO LIKES BRUSSELS SPROUTS?

Of all the vegetables I loathed as a child, and there were dozens, Brussels sprouts topped the list. I was an incredibly finicky eater, gagging on 90% of the food I was expected to eat. Neither threats nor bribes could tempt me to swallow such items as liver, cheese (even cream cheese) and just about any cooked vegetable but corn and peas.

What is it that makes one child willing to eat anything and another balk at even the most innocuous menu? I was spunky and adventurous (some might say naughty) as a kid, but when it came to food, my sense of adventure curdled as fast as my stomach. It was only when I married Hank that my taste buds grew up and realized what they'd been missing.

Out of three daughters, the last was the only one to be a picky eater. With my background of experience, I was all for ignoring the problem, but Hank was brought up on the rule that children had to try at least one bite of everything on the menu. Tam, like me, would stubbornly refuse to take even the one bite. Now, however, she adores everything from Cajun cooking to venison.

Out of five grandchildren, only Tam's son Ridley is a seriously fussy eater. Fortunately, the one vegetable he likes is broccoli, so that is what Tam gives him, almost every night. Knowing that her own palate matured eventually, she has no rules, no "Just One Bite," no members of "The Clean Plate Club," no bribes or punishments.

Since Ridley likes broccoli, he might well like Brussels sprouts if they came directly from the garden. These two cousins look just alike as seedlings. They both have two grayish green leaves similar in shape and only as they mature are they easy to tell apart.

I was sold a flat of sprouts mislabeled broccoli early in my gardening career. When I discovered what was occupying precious garden space I was furious. Visions of the gray, gaseous, overcooked sprouts I'd tried to foist onto my dog or my classmates sogged into my mind as the tiny cabbages appeared above each broad leaf.

Thrift required me to harvest them, but it was their deliciousness that made me freeze the excess and continue growing Brussels sprouts in future years. Being able to pick a green vegetable when everything else in the garden is frost-blackened and dead is a treat. Some years we've had fresh Brussels sprouts in December.

If you're not fond of this vegetable, you might just try growing it in your garden anyway. It is vastly superior to the sprouts in the supermarket, which are rarely harvested after cold weather arrives when they're at their best. I plant my seeds directly in the garden in June, as I know I won't begin harvesting until late October. If you buy seedlings, plant them two feet apart. They grow up, not out. They can be set out as late as July.

The apical tip of each plant produces a hormone that inhibits growth of the axillary buds, which are the sprouts. As the plant grows, the lower buds are less affected by this hormone and begin to mature. Cut off the apical tip just as the lower sprouts begin to mature and you eliminate the growth-inhibiting hormone, forcing all the sprouts to ripen at once, handy if you're planning to freeze them.

Your kids may turn up their noses, even if your Brussels sprouts are home grown, but if they're fussy eaters, please don't make them choke them down. Forcing is a waste of everyone's time, and usually proves that kids have more perseverance than their parents. The inhibiting hormone deep inside those picky eaters cannot be eliminated by making them swallow foods they don't like. When they grow up, that hormone will undoubtedly vanish on its own.

FREE FERTILIZER

How I love getting something for nothing. Right now I'm huddled by the woodstove, but at the same time I'm creating some free fertilizer – wood ashes. Whether you have an open fireplace, an old-fashioned Franklin or a modern airtight, those brightly burning oak and ash and maple logs adding pleasure to cold winter evenings eventually result in woodashes, an excellent fertilizer. They contain 1.5% phosphorus and at least 7 % potassium.

My ashes also contain dozens of cigarette foil papers and hundreds of small plastic filters. If you're fortunate enough to live in a house without smokers, your ashes may only contain a bit of tinfoil from candy bars or margarine, a spent flashbulb or two, and possibly a melted plastic bottle from the medicine cabinet. If any of the above items are so numerous as to be offensive, they can be screened out through a piece of hardware cloth before the ashes are spread on the lawn or garden.

Since I am not a meticulous person, I don't sift my ashes any more than I skin tomatoes for the salad or move furniture when I vacuum. Those foreign objects don't hurt plants, and the unsightly ones can be picked up later when they offend the eye. If you are the meticulous type, sift your ashes on a windless day or you'll find yourself looking as gray as a three-day-old snowfall in Manhattan.

Although nitrogen is the most important nutrient plants use, phosphorus and potassium, the two found in woodash, are second and third on the list of importance. Phosphorus provides plants with strong growth and a good root system. Without it they will have stunted growth and poor fruit.

Potassium strengthens stems, the reason it is enjoyed by long-legged delphiniums and wobbly-headed peonies. It also improves the keeping quality of vegetables, so carrots and potatoes that must try to stay crisp and bright through a dreary winter spent in the dark cold cellar like it.

Wood ashes, which are sweet, tend to improve New England soils, which are sour. If you're not familiar with the terms sweet and sour, may I say they have nothing to do with pork. Sweet is alkaline and a high pH, while sour is acid and a low pH.

The pH scale goes from 0 to 14, ascending from very acidic or sour soil through neutral (7.0) to alkaline or sweet soil. Unlike a scale that measures pounds and ounces, this scale is logarithmic - each step of the scale is multiplied by 10, just like the Richter scale that measures the seismic vibrations of an earthquake.

If you put two babies on a regular scale and one's gained a pound or two and the other one has lost, you might not notice much difference, but try putting those babies on a pH scale. The baby who's lost weight would be so sour he'd be unbearable to live with, while the baby who'd gained weight would be the cuddliest, most appealing tot you've ever laid eyes on, all sweetness.

And what does pH stand for? "The Potential of Hydrogen." Hydrogen is a colorless, highly flammable gas and is the most abundant element in the universe. It's what blew up the Hindenburg. Most dirigibles, blimps, zeppelins or whatever you want to call them, use helium, but the United States didn't allow the export of this gas during World War II so the Germans used hydrogen, with rather disastrous results.

Some plants like lots of hydrogen and others don't. Vegetables such as radishes, watermelons, corn, eggplants, peas, peppers, tomatoes and parsnips like a pH from 4.0 to 6.0. Others, such as asparagus, beets, broccoli, Brussels sprouts, cauliflower, carrots, lettuce, onions and spinach prefer a pH of 7.0 to 7.5. Most perennials like a neutral pH, but shrubs such as azaleas, yews, laurel and rhododendrons like an acid soil.

A soil test kit will give you an accurate reading of the pH, but the best way to neutralize your soil is to add plenty of organic matter, which acts to control either excess alkalinity or excess acidity. Whichever way the soil is bad, adding lots of compost will tend to correct it.

I usually spread our accumulated ashes when Mother Natures dishes up one of those balmy March afternoons when I just *have* to get outside. I feel like Lady Bountiful delivering food to the poor as I dole out ashes to the various plants. I walk down the perennial border, giving large scoopfuls of ash to the delphiniums and the peonies. Both of these plants dislike acid, and I can almost hear them sigh with relief as the soft cool ashes ease their aching feet.

I also sprinkle ashes around the lilacs and the clematis vines, the asparagus and the raspberries, and if I had roses, the roses. If I still have ashes left over, and I usually do, I dump them on the compost pile, which is easy, or, assuming my energy level is sufficient, I put them in a large trash bag, poke a few holes in the bottom, and drift up and down the lawn like Ophelia, trailing ashes in my wake.

A REAL JANUARY THAW

What's your favorite month? April, delighting us with the first signs of spring? June, the perfect month for weddings? September, in its glorious coat of many colors? How about your *least* favorite month? Of course it's the weather in each month that usually makes us love or hate it. Here, in The Icebox of Connecticut, January is the month we like the least.

If we could shrink the universe until our planet was the size and weight of a Ping-Pong ball, the sun would measure some twelve and a half feet in diameter and weigh about three tons! Yet in New England its rays can hardly melt an icicle at this time of year.

The sun ceases its retreat to the Southern hemisphere on December 21st and starts climbing north again, but we're still starting our days in the dark and only gain 20 minutes of daylight in January. About the only aspect of this month I look forward to is the usual January thaw. No one seems to know why New England manages to have this whiff of spring in three out of every four years, but it is a delight when it occurs.

A true January thaw gives us Hope with a capital H. It means walking outside in short sleeves. The few piles of unmelted snow sparkle in the sun. The ice in the pond groans and rumbles. The meadows, flattened by December's snow, are as smooth and tawny as the deer who stand like invisible statues in them.

The first winter we spent on Locust Hill, we had a thaw I will never forget. I'd just brought Hank home from the hospital where he'd undergone kidney surgery (he manages to have major surgery every ten years or so.) The little rill of water leading to the pond that dries up every July and doesn't appear again until spring was a torrent, pouring a sheet of water over the entire lawn.

The pond wasn't even a year old, but fortunately the dam had a well-rooted stand of grass growing on it and seemed to be holding firm against the tide of water enveloping it. The spillway was a different story. Slowly but surely the pressure of water racing across it was carrying its soil away in a brown deluge into the lower pasture.

In constructing the spillway, we'd buried an old iron gate in it to serve as rip-rap. The gate was still frozen in place, but the water, refusing to be delayed in its rush out of the pond, was ignoring this minor obstruction and was ravenously tearing away at the dirt below the gate.

The rain was coming down from the sky as fast as water was escaping from the pond. Talk about putting your finger in the dike! If something wasn't done soon there'd be an empty pond by the end of the day. Hank, in no shape to solve this impending catastrophe, called our neighbor, Bob Jacquier, for help.

Within minutes Bob had arrived on his backhoe. He attached a chain to the old iron gate and after an agonizing five minutes, managed to break it loose from the winter's icy grip. His wife Dot and their four children, plus me and my three, totally drenched by the downpour, began lugging rocks to the spillway as Bob scooped up dirt with the backhoe from nearby and dumped it into the gaping hole.

At first it appeared we were in a losing battle, but then slowly our accumulated rocks began to take hold, slowing the roar of water that was so eager to escape. What a sight we made, slipping and slithering in the mud, our boots squelching water, our hands wet and raw from carrying rocks. Poor Hank watched from the front window, helpless to do anything but make hot cocoa in preparation for our return.

Now that was a real January thaw! Frankly, I prefer the ones that arrive just bringing sunshine.

WHAT MAKES A GREEN THUMB?

I'm not big on the supernatural, but last week I was given a book called <u>Psychic Exploration</u> and found the chapter on man-plant communication pretty interesting. The first section describing the experiments done by Cleve Backster I was actually familiar with as PBS recently had a "Nova" program about them. He was the polygraph expert who attached his machine's electrodes to a philodendron leaf to see what reactions would show up on the graph.

A polygraph used on a human being records changes in breathing, blood pressure and pulse rate, as well as something called galvanic skin response (GSR). Backster decided to try burning Phil with a match, since most changes in GSR are triggered by a "threat to well-being."

At the instant of decision, the tracing pattern made by the recording pen zoomed upward, the sort of response one might get if Lizzie Borden were hooked up to the machine and asked if she'd used her Daddy's ax on August 4, 1902. Poor Phil's GSR went sky high at the mere thought of being burned. Pretty amazing, isn't it? Mind-reading plants!

The chapter next described the strange phenomena occurring in Findhorn, a small community on the edge of the North Sea. The soil there is so barren it should support next to nothing, yet it produces dozens of healthy flowers, vegetables and trees of miraculous size. How can the people of Findhorn raise 40-pound cabbages and huge flowers that normally wouldn't even survive in that climate?

The British Soil Association is unable to explain it, but the villagers have no trouble. They believe angelic beings control the growth of their plants. They leave an untouched portion of their garden for the angels in gratitude. They also spend much time talking to their plants, praising their beauty and size.

Although the scientific community scorned the Rev. Franklin Loehr's experiment with flower seeds, I found it quite believable. He started seeds in two separate flower beds, giving each bed identical sunlight, water and soil. He prayed over one flower bed daily and left the other to the devil. Need I say that the churchgoing flowers grew to gigantic proportions while the heretics barely bloomed?

The book included studies in man-plant communication that were more scientific, but it seems they all prove what gardeners the world over have known all along - a green thumb is nothing more than a love of growing things that communicates itself to the plants being cared for.

After I finished reading about all these mind-reading plants, I went out to start tidying up the perennial border for the winter. I use neither trowel nor clipper for this job, finding it quicker and easier to just use my hands. I hate wearing those stiff, ungainly garden gloves, so I buy nice-fitting dress gloves at the thrift store. They're very comfortable and seem to protect my hands adequately. I feel a little silly as I step out the back door in bluejeans, sweat shirt and white gloves, but now that I'm aware of how plants can feel, I like to think they enjoy being handled with such elegance.

That afternoon, however, working in the garden was fraught with anxiety. Every time I started to rip out the spreading purple stems of an over-eager beebalm or toss a tired-looking patch of forget-me-not into the garden cart, I felt I had to stop and apologize to them. I was constantly talking to this flower or that, complimenting, cajoling, explaining. The clean-up job took a lot longer than it usually does, but I think we all had a good time.

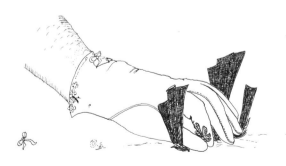

The month of January is usually what I call "See-Through Time," when the roadside woods are bare of leaves and undergrowth, but not buried in snowdrifts. It's amazing how far you can see and how clearly the contours of a woodland are defined. Granite ledges and boulders become conspicuous. So do old woods roads or a swamp full of cattails. A secret pond never seen before glints in the winter sunlight beyond the curtain of trees.

A stand of oaks still clinging to their rust-colored leaves or a cluster of young beech saplings still holding on to their pale yellow ones, is easily identified at this time of year. Driveways that in summer lead to unseen houses can be followed by the eye to reveal a modern mansion, a turreted monster or a mobile home.

Sometimes I'll spot the old caved-in foundation of a house or a circle of flat stones topping an abandoned well; at others I'll recognize an orchard, the gnarled branches of ancient apple trees once enjoying the space and freedom to reach the sun now crowded out by new forest growth. A brook hidden in summer by lush green undergrowth makes a black ribbon between its white snowbanks, seen clearly beyond the screen of bare tree trunks.

All sorts of things catch the eye – two men sawing timber, the still statue of a deer, the messy twigs of a crow's nest high up in an ash tree. Once I saw a dilapidated tree house with a rope ladder perched in the crotch of a huge white oak.

But what sparks my imagination most is the sight of one of those old stone walls tumbling across a wooded hillside. Those rocky boundaries once surrounded open land. It boggles the mind to think what it must have been like to clear an acre of woodland back then. New England was almost entirely forest when our forefathers settled here.

Before a farmer could build that stone wall or the foundation for his house, he had to saw down hundreds of trees with nothing but a crosscut saw.

What a monumental task! I've sawed down plenty of tree limbs with a handsaw in my day, and even though most were smaller than my arm, that arm ached before I was through. I'm sure our forefathers were coping with trees far larger than their aching bodies. At least they had the satisfaction of needing what they cut – oak and chestnut for house beams, locust and cedar for fence posts, maple for furniture, ash for handles, and just about any variety of hardwood for the wood stove.

Once the trees had been cut down and the wood carted away, what was left was a giant stubble of tree stumps, their roots tenaciously clinging to life. In the days without power equipment, uprooting a viable tree stump would have been almost as hard as prying your husband out of his chair when he's watching the Superbowl. And without modern herbicides, finding a way to kill the stump took more imagination than figuring how to get rid of an interfering mother-in-law.

Rubbing off the new sprouts that appeared around the stump eventually took the life out of even the most stubborn stump, but it took several years. Once they were dead and pulled out with a logging chain, there was the back-breaking task of picking rocks. I suppose a horse and a stone boat and a passel of children took on the job of the more manageable rocks while Dad uprooted the donics (an old Yankee term for huge rocks). During my See-Through Time I've spotted some humungous boulders fitted into those old stone walls.

Next time you're driving on a back road and spy an old stone wall staggering between the trees or threading its way along a wooded hillside, picture what it must have looked like in the 1800s – an open hay field, a cow pasture, the boundary of a homestead.

Since I'm the sort of penny pincher who NEVER runs the dishwasher until every space is filled, and then rushes to turn it off before the dry cycle, you'd think I'd be the sort of gardener who wouldn't dream of paying a nursery for seedlings I could raise myself. Back when I started gardening, however, a flat of broccoli was as cheap as a gallon of gas. Consequently it was only when inflation forced the price of nursery seedlings to grow faster than the seedlings themselves, that I began raising my own.

It was strictly a monetary decision, so it was a shock to discover the fun I'd been missing. Being able to get my hands into rich friable soil instead of sulking over the oil bill or the cost of airfares to Jamaica was a delight. Besides the joy of feeling cool earth beneath my fingers and the excitement of watching tiny cotyledons (a seed's first leaves) push up into the light, I became experienced in handling delicate plants and understanding their growth habits.

Plant nurseries offer a vast selection of growing mediums - potting soil, peat moss, perlite, just to name the "Ps". Most of them resemble sawdust or shredded Styrofoam, which takes away some of the fun, but they do have one big advantage - they're sterile. If you use home-grown dirt as I do, the result may be the Big Bac Attack called "damping off".

I'd heard of this dreadful disease, but not until I saw it wipe out all my flats of baby seedlings did I believe in it. It has been compared to whooping cough as it only attacks children, but I consider it on a par with crib death. It may be preventable, but never curable. To sterilize your soil, bake it in the oven at 200 degrees for an hour.

A word of warning - one year I filled the roasting pan with dirt from the bushel I'd been storing in the cellar since fall, put it in the oven and ten minutes later hastily took it out again. Our cat obviously preferred my potting soil to her Kitty Litter! After airing the house, I went and bought some nice clean dirt.

Styrofoam cups, milk cartons or aluminum trays make good seedling containers, but be sure and poke holes in them for good ventilation and drainage. The shallower the container, the faster seeds will germinate, and the faster they will need transplanting.

Seeds need warm soil (65 or 70 degrees) to germinate, but my seedlings live in the guestroom which rarely gets above 50 so I provide them with an electric blanket. All the flats are placed on an old enameled kitchen tabletop salvaged from the dump that sits upside-down on the blanket. Its one-inch lip allows me to water from below.

Once the seeds have sprouted, the blanket is turned from high to low, and a double fluorescent light is propped about six inches above the seedlings. It's left on day and night, but the plants don't seem to resent being expected to work 24 hours a day. With their feet warm, but the air cool, they grow into nice, thick-stemmed, well-rooted plants.

The last step before seedlings face the real world is the cold frame, known as the half-way house, where they are "hardened off" for a few weeks, getting used to the cold. Seedlings that have been raised from birth in a cool environment need little adjustment and will quickly adapt to their final home in the garden.

THAT FIRST REAL SPRING DAY

Scientists may label March 21st the first day of spring, but just because the sun hits its midpoint on that day doesn't necessarily mean balmy weather is upon us. To me spring is only for real on the morning you walk outside without a sweater and spend the day racing around from one garden chore to another like a kid in a toy store.

This year I had to wait until half-past April to get the kind of delicious day I'm talking about. I was tidying up the kitchen that morning and as I took the garbage out to the compost pile, I realized spring had sprung. The daffodils on the knoll were all in bloom. The mother ewes stalked down the lane to see if my compost contributions contained any lettuce or carrot peelings. The twin lambs, less than a week old and baa-ing nervously, bounced down the lane like two rubber balls to find their mother.

The air was soft as velvet and kitchen duty forgotten as I watched a third baby lamb get butted by old Aunt Gertrude, a barren ewe no longer interested in children. With a small bleat the lamb rambled over to his proper mother and punched her swollen udder. His stiff front legs collapsed and his tail began wiggling in ecstasy.

I looked around at fields turned green almost overnight, the pond mirror-blue and brimming, the maple buds crimson and ready to burst. And everywhere I turned I saw something that needed doing – the lawns dotted with broken twigs, old bones and even less attractive items left by the dogs through the winter; the English ivy seared brown and brittle on the front retaining wall; new strawberry leaves trying to push off their pine needle covers.

"Where will I begin? I ought to pull the mulch off the strawberries, move the seedlings out to the cold frame. Oh, and clean out the birdbaths and houses before the tree swallows return from the South. But let's check out the new tulips first."

I latched the gate and hurried out to the perennial border, whispering my list of priorities. I'm sure lots of folks talk to themselves when they're alone, but for some weird reason I don't talk, I whisper. Who is going to hear me?

The tulip buds were still hiding in their green cocoons, but all sorts of other goodies were poking through the earth. I knelt down and pulled up a sprawling chickweed, and before I knew it an hour had vanished and a pile of pulled weeds had accumulated.

"Get your garden gloves, dummy," I whispered, looking at my muddy fingers, "and a trowel, too, while you're at it." But on the way to the shed I spotted the wiry remains of last year's thyme between the flagstones and got the scissors instead, intending to just trim the thyme a little.

"GET YOUR GLOVES!" (not whispered) as my fingers dug around the roots of the third tuft of grass growing in the thyme. But inside the shed I spotted the new edger Hank had given me for Christmas, and couldn't resist just trying it out for a little minute which turned into 15. I spent the entire day that way, just like a kid on a carousel, dashing from one tempting horse to the next.

When I finally got my gloves from the shed I remembered the flats of seedlings still sitting in the house. The broccoli could go directly into the garden, and the tomatoes too, if I could find my "Wall-o-water" protectors. "Oops, better get the garden gates back up first or you'll have the dogs right here helping you plant."

The gates were in the shed, but I forgot them and the seedlings in the excitement of another lamb. The last ewe had finally given birth. From what I could see it looked like a baby girl, her ears two black spears jutting out from a silly triangle face. "Still damp and wobbly, but definitely perky," I whispered, but no one heard me but the sheep.

THE DAM RAMS

We've always run a small flock of scrub sheep on Locust Hill – four or five ewes of mixed origin, plus a ram. Although the ram's primary function is to make sure his wives get pregnant, he is also expected to keep the grass on the pond dam trimmed all summer and is consequently referred to as the dam ram.

In the more than 20 years we've lived on the hill, we've had a variety of rams, and if you think lawn mowers are temperamental, you should try a dam ram. Like a lot of males, they can be hard-headed creatures. Most get their kicks from butting people. Since walking in a pasture inhabited by such an animated sledgehammer is about as much fun as riding bumper cars with a bad back, we take the ram away from his girls the minute the grass reaches an edible height and stake him on the dam to play lawn mower.

Our first dam ram was a grass-guzzling brute we called Rammit, as he would charge anything that moved – dogs, chickens, bumblebees. The only way I could move his stake was by putting a bucket of grain at the outermost reach of both the old and new tether areas. Then, if I was quick enough, I could pound the stake in its new hole before Rammit could finish and knock over the bucket and me.

That summer was dry and rainless, and each time I moved Rammit's stake, I grew more frantic and fumbling in my hurry to get the job done. Finally I decided I'd rather mow the dam myself, and since Rammit belonged to a neighboring farmer, I sent him home.

The next spring I really didn't want to mow the steep bank around the pond myself (as I've probably already said, Hank doesn't mow lawns,) so I tethered a ewe on the dam, leaving her lamb free to frolic nearby. A week later she was dead. The vet claimed she'd eaten too much lush grass and died of colic, but I suspected she'd died of apoplexy just watching her baby cavort around the pond unattended.

Our 8-year-old Bridget volunteered to be the orphaned lamb's mother. She named him Zinnia, bottled and babied him and begged us not to turn him into lamb chops come fall. Luckily we'd only docked his tail (how could we bear to do more to such a sweet pet?), so we agreed to let him be the new father of our flock.

The only trouble was that Zinnia thought he was a person, not a sheep. Instead of charging lustily after his new wives when it came time for his marital duties, he stood at the pasture gate all day blatting for Bridget. We never did spot any sexual activity in the pasture that winter, but unless you believe in Immaculate Conception, Zinnia must have done his job as there was the proper complement of lambs in the spring. I suppose he felt that such amours should occur out of sight behind the barn.

Since our flock was down to three ewes, we decided to replace Zinnia's dead mother with two of his daughters. This meant that come fall, incest would be rampant, but there was no thought of getting rid of such a biddable lawn mower. Zinnia, however, was obviously more bothered by his incestuous life than we were. He grew very cranky, backing off and lowering his head at anyone's approach.

The next winter we hired a young kid named Tinker to feed dogs, cats, sheep and chickens while we were on a family vacation, but asked our good friend Henny if she'd water the houseplants and collect the eggs. Each morning Henny would stop on her way to work and search out the eggs laid by our roaming chickens. One day she spotted a few eggs in the sheep manger, innocently opened the inner door and collected them. The next thing she knew she was laid out in the muck with a tongue-panting Zinnia leering down at her. She escaped with no serious damage, unless you consider going to the office with runs in your stockings, manure on your skirt and egg on your face damaging.

Henny hadn't stopped to close the door as she fled, so when Tinker zoomed into the yard on his motorcycle that afternoon, KABOOM! He found himself zooming around the yard on foot, chased by a snorting Zinnia. Tinker's reaction was not fright, but fury. Once over his surprise, he raced to his motorcycle, hopped on and gunned it straight at his opponent. The chase was reversed and Tinker pursued Zinnia until the ram was as worn out as an old wool sweater.

After hearing Henny's lurid tale of being almost raped by a ram, we decided we'd better sell Zinnia, but before we could find a buyer he followed in his mother's hoofprints. This time the vet claimed death was due to heat prostration. That was just the vet's idea of a joke (sheep don't die from heat prostration,) but not realizing this fact, we felt guilty that we'd tethered him on the dam in the hot sun without a speck of shade.

The following winter we were discussing the problem with friends and puzzling over what sort of trees to plant to provide shade for future rams. Gene offered the perfect solution, a large pink beach umbrella. He'd bought this item to take on a vacation, but when he appeared on the beach his family had been so convulsed with laughter at the sight of Father mincing across the hot sand carrying this fringed and flowered oversized parasol that he quietly put it away in the garage on his return home.

The gift of this elegant umbrella made getting another dam ram a must, but we searched until we found a truly docile one named Beaver. We planned to change his moniker as soon as we'd come up with a better one, but this new dam ram fell in the pond the first day and nearly drowned. The kids spotted him floundering in the shallow water, his wet wool weighing him down so he was blowing bubbles in the mud. As we pulled him out we all agreed he should keep his original name.

Beaver was a very well endowed ram. In fact he was so spectacularly equipped that if he wasn't careful he'd step on his own equipment. He stood around looking sheepish and never charged or butted anyone, but his progeny were a sickly lot. In two years we'd forgotten the dangers of having a virulent father, and decided we should upgrade the flock by buying a quality ram.

Soccer, by Low Cost Hill standards, was an expensive ram, but he was also magnificent. His proud stance as he posed under the pink umbrella made his price tag almost worth it, and he wasn't too aggressive, so long as you were carrying a baseball bat.

Soccer was a mere lightweight, however, compared to the next dam ram we acquired. At first, when not on a tether, Jammer spent all his time battering down fences, and we spent most of ours repairing them. It wasn't until that winter that we found him a substitute that eliminated the problem. We filled a strong metal bucket with a dozen big stones and hung it by a chain in the barn.

Jammer used the bucket as a punching bag. He spent most evenings practicing on it. He'd get a 4- or 5-foot running start and charge the bucket full tilt, sometimes hitting it solidly enough to send it bouncing wildly off the barn wall. The first few times he bashed the bucket in the middle of the night, we woke up thinking the house was under attack, but we became used to the noise and found it much less aggravating than replacing fences.

DOGWOOD TREES

Half the fun of garden projects is anticipating their completion. Looking forward to the day when a plant will bloom, a newly seeded lawn will be green or a flower bed will fill in can sometimes be the best part, especially if what you're anticipating never comes to pass.

When we first moved to East Canaan, I was told by a local nurseryman that dogwoods rarely bloom in this area. The buds of these handsome edge trees, formed in the fall, can't survive the frigid temperatures of a Berkshire winter. So even though dogwoods were my favorite trees, I decided not to waste my money buying one.

Ten years later I came across a huge dogwood in bloom while walking in our woods. Looking closely, I identified a dozen seedlings growing beneath its sheltering limbs. They were perfect transplanting size, and not only free for the taking, but hopefully as hardy as their happily blooming mother. Within a week I'd moved two to the backyard.

Those two saplings grew into very shapely trees, but it took many years before I spotted a multitude of swollen buds on them. With renewed anticipation, I sat through the winter's sub-zero temperatures, wondering if my dogwood buds would live to tell the tale.

The following May a shower of white stars burst forth. In fact both dogwoods bloomed every spring for another ten years. In really cold winters a few buds got frostbite, but the ones that survived seemed that much more special. Putting a single branch of blooms in a vase against a dark background made me feel on a par with the most artistic Japanese flower arranger.

What you and I would like to call the petals of a dogwood blossom are not petals at all, but bracts. What does it matter, except possibly to the insects who pollinate the tiny cluster of greenish white flowers they surround. By the end of summer this same cluster has become brilliant red berries that usually remain on the branches through much of the winter.

There is no flowering tree that is shapelier than the dogwood, but recently it has been attacked by a fatal disease, dogwood dieback. The fungus *discula* has been identified as the culprit doing the killing, but a cure for this scourge of the tree world has yet to be found.

A dogwood's first symptoms are inconspicuous, small, purple-rimmed spots on the foliage of lower branches. Then small twigs on these branches begin to die, turning tan and dry at the tips. These dead twigs result in clusters of waterspouts that appear on the trunk and lower limbs the same way they might if the tree had been heavily pruned. Once the waterspouts become infected, cankers develop at their bases and in a few years this dread disease has spread to upper branches.

The *discula* fungus belongs to a group of tree diseases known as anthracnoses, and is spread by spores. Dead leaves and twigs harbor these spores, which are carried up to higher branches by wind or splashing rain. Spraying a sick dogwood with fungicide can help stave off their spread. Pruning the watersprouts, raking up fallen leaves and removing infected leaves that have not fallen, will all improve a dogwood's chance of survival, especially if these practices are done in the early stages.

I had high hopes that my dogwoods were living in such a clean environment that they'd never get dieback, but eventually they began to show signs that they were infected. Since they had also grown tall enough to put shadows on the vegetable garden, I cut them down.

Eventually I bought a Kousa dogwood, a variety that isn't susceptible to dieback, but its shape is not half as attractive as its cousin's.

VEGETABLE TIPS

Planted your peas yet? Tradition says you can plant on St. Patrick's Day in New England, but I don't love mucking about in such cold muddy weather. Pea vines are as brave as Admiral Byrd about the cold, surviving even at 20 degrees, but I prefer to plant my collection of wizened little faces in mid-April when spring is in the air.

The one year I did plant my peas in March I felt like a faithful dog waiting for his dead master to appear. After about a month I finally assumed my little marvels had turned to mush and I replanted. A week later – you guessed it – both batches poked through the warm soil together.

Lettuce is another crop that can tolerate pretty cold temperatures. In fact it doesn't like hot weather at all.

Miss Lettuce is a debutante deserving of a ballad.
She does not quickly run to seed,
Is very popular indeed
In any social salad.
In June when she is coming out
Miss Lettuce can resist the drought.

Miss Lettuce has the biggest heart in all the kitchen garden,
Be sure to pick her in her prime
For if she isn't picked in time
Her heart is apt to harden.
You'll find her at her best, I mean
When she is very young and green.

Reginal Arkell, one of the few poets to write about such mundane things as vegetables, wrote the above. He paints a very demure picture of Miss Lettuce, but she can be right with the times as she matures. That bitter milky fluid in old lettuce plants is actually a narcotic. It was once used as a substitute for opium and is almost as potent as marijuana.

You don't have to have a garden to enjoy fresh lettuce. My mom, who's 87 and looks about 8 (she weighs only 70 pounds), grows hers in a red wagon. She drilled drainage holes in the four corners, filled the wagon with potting soil mixed with lime (lettuce likes a high pH) and plants a tiny corner with lettuce seed every few weeks, transplanting the seedlings into rows when they are finger high.

The wagon is an ideal container since lettuce does best in cool weather. On hot August days Mom wheels her wagon to shady places in the yard, around to the faucet for easy watering, but best of all, right inside the back porch when Jack Frost is expected to return from his summer vacation.

I've always grown several rows of carrots in the garden, as Eeyore, our burro, eats whatever we don't. Carrot seeds are tiny and hard to handle so I mix them with a cup or two of sand. That makes them easier to spread and also helps eliminate weeds. I add a few zinnia seeds to help mark the row as carrots take forever to germinate. To hurry them up I put a kettle on the stove while I'm planting, then pour the boiling water on the newly planted seeds. I didn't believe this trick when I read about it, so the first time I did only half the row and was amazed to see it full of greenery a week earlier than the other half.

My carrots tend to be hairy. All those little side roots are caused by too much manure in the soil. It's also what makes my potatoes scabby. Since I peel most of the potatoes and give the hairiest carrots to Eeyore, who doesn't seem to mind their whiskery state, I've refused to give up manure.

I learned the hard way that a row of zucchini is enough to feed an army. This vegetable produces green babies as prolifically as a frog lays eggs. Giving space to more than two plants in the garden is a mistake. If you're a Yankee who believes in "Waste not, want not" you'll be forced to eat the result not only as a vegetable but in salads, soup, bread, relish (great on hot-dogs) or give it to the sheep.

Since I like baking as much as I like cleaning the oven, I never made zucchini bread until the summer our first daughter got married. Our kids, like their mom, dislike anything "store-bought," and Trum wanted a homemade wedding cake, not white or yellow or chocolate, but one made with zucchini. Fortunately this plan was hatched the summer before the wedding so I had no problem filling the freezer with bags and bags of grated zucchini.

We took the basic bread recipe, added extra sugar and spices, lots more raisins and nuts, and baked enough to make a four-tiered wedding cake covered in white frosting. It was such a success that we duplicated it for both Bridget's and Tam's weddings.

Have you ever tasted a Vidalia? This famous onion is so controversial that Georgia finally passed a law allowing only onions grown in the area surrounding the town of Vidalia to be given this illustrious title.

Unlike these fabulously sweet onions, my onions always left me in tears, literally and figuratively. It was only a few years ago that I found out why. When you crush or cut an onion, sulfur compounds are released which irritate your nose and eyes. The less sulfur, the less crying, and the sweeter the onion. Vidalia onions, like many other varieties, are grown from Yellow Granex hybrid seed, but only when this variety is raised in the sulfur-free soil around Vidalia, Georgia, is it so sweet and tear-free it can be eaten raw like an apple.

In recent years some strong, but sweet competition has appeared - the Walla Walla, from the state of Washington; the Maui, raised in the volcanic soils of Hawaii; the Texas 1015, and California's Imperial Sweet. Notice something missing? The Northeast doesn't seem to be joining the competition. That's because the Granex hybrids on which all these sweet no-tear onions are based won't grow well in a "long day" climate.

The Granex-type onions like to form bulbs when the days are only 12 hours long, but in the East that occurs only in spring when the ground is too cool for bulbing. When the days get warm enough, they also get too long, and the result is tough, pungent onions. Horticulturists have just recently managed to create a new hybrid onion, "Sweet Sandwich" that actually thrives on 16 hours of daylight.

I grew these hybrids last summer and they really were sweet and delicious. If your onions make you cry, try the Sweet Sandwich variety.

My children learned how vegetables grow as soon as they could toddle out to the garden and help pick the beans, but I can remember one summer when I had the pleasure of introducing a city child to the miracle of gardening.

Tommy was about four at the time and his blue eyes grew as big as morning glories when we went out to pick a ripe tomato for lunch. After all, tomatoes are supposed to be in cellophane cartons, not hanging like red rubber balls on green vines. He was as delighted as a kid at a magic show as I showed him around the garden, and I must admit I felt a bit like Houdini myself.

I pulled aside the leaves of a squash plant to reveal a tiny golden sausage just starting life, and another, fatter than the biceps of a weight lifter, that I'd neglected to pick when it was young. We walked the new carrot row, thinning a few so that he could see the magic of pulling a bright orange carrot from the dirt. We poked among the giant pumpkin leaves to find the fat green babies hiding in the shade. I even untied the leaves of a cauliflower plant, relishing Tommy's laughter as he discovered the little golf ball tucked inside.

Unfortunately the pea vines were just dried-up old women no longer producing, but the bush beans were heavy with ripe string beans ready for picking. I went to get a basket, and what with the telephone ringing and a few other interruptions, it was a while before I got back to the garden. Sweet little Tommy had turned into a magician himself. He had pulled the entire row of inch-long carrots out of the hat so to speak, and was busy turning baby beets into wilted piles of debris.

Well, there are easier ways to teach a child about the joys of gardening. Letting him have a garden of his own is one of the best. I was given a row in my family's Victory Garden when I was a kid. I grew radishes, my favorite food back then, and carrots, which I also liked, provided they weren't cooked. I kept a salt shaker at the end of the row.

Our daughter Trum's first attempt at gardening was a gourd house. We made a teepee of sturdy poles and Trum planted a seed beside each one. Gourd vines are easy to grow and excellent climbers. By late summer Trum had a cool and shady teepee, dripping curiously shaped, striped and multicolored gourds. She varnished the best ones to use as decorations at Thanksgiving.

The next daughter, Bridget, grew an Indian corn in her first garden, its kernels a bright mix of blues, reds, whites and yellows. It, too, was duly varnished and, along with the gourds, came out of the attic each Thanksgiving until the mice had a little feast of their own with it.

When Tam, our last little girl, decided she wanted a garden, she insisted on growing nothing but peanuts, despite being warned that they needed a far longer growing season than we had in our area. An early frost ruined the whole crop. Peanuts have a long and complicated method of producing seeds. The plant has two sets of flowers, one for show and one for growing peanuts. Once the fertile flowers have been pollinated, they send out peduncles – that's right, peduncles – that bend over, then bury their tips in the ground and produce seeds – peanuts. So there's the sex life of a peanut in a nutshell. No wonder they need a long, hot season.

Other plants that are fun for kids to try are sunflowers, pumpkins and potatoes. I guess I should have shown young Tommy my potato patch that day. He would have had a super time digging them up and I could have made potato salad instead of carrot soup for dinner that night.

Before your child or grandchild discovers what a delight it is to dig things up, give him a trowel and some seed packets and let him dig things in. Who know, he may end up being a second James Crockett.

47

ANTHROPOMORPHIC VEGETABLES

The vegetables were arguing
Which one of them was best,
Which had the most achievements,
Which was the tastiest.
The beautiful asparagus spoke up the first of all.
"I may be past my prime, my dears,
But no one grows as tall."
"Aw, shucks," the corn grinned down at her,
"I guess I shouldn't boast,
But my old stalk can stretch beyond
The highest garden post."
A ripe but shy tomato said,
"I'm fancy and high-bred.
I love the heat, it makes me sweet."
She blushed a rosy red.
The Swiss chard leaf began to curl
And yodel at the sky.
"My stem gets cut right at the butt,
Yet still I multiply."
"We're very fresh and tender, too,"
The baby onions cried.
"I think you're fresh and impudent,"
Miss Broccoli replied.

"Such bickering!" Aunt Lettuce moaned,
"I think my head will split.
We'll never figure out who's best
'Til we calm down a bit."
The mealy-mouthed potato wailed,
"I've got the scabs this year.
I've had no starch since early March."
He shed a milky tear.
"Oh, wipe your eyes," an old beet said,
"At least you're not too plump.
If I continue gaining weight
They'll throw me on the dump."
The cucumber let out a burp,
"My indigestion's bad.
I guess it must have been that dose
Of garden lime I had."
The carrot plants got all choked up —
It really was absurd —
Their heads were buried in the sand
So none of them was heard.
Poor Mr. Celery tried to speak,
His skin a sickly white.
His voice was just a whisper 'cause
His collar was too tight.
"Pipe down!" the red hot radish yelled,
"Pipe down, you silly clods."
And each young pea laughed out with glee,
And nearly split their pods.
Then Grandpa Cauliflower coughed
And shook his snow-white head.
"I think we've bickered long enough.
Let's get to work," he said.
The vegetables all dug right in,
Their argument forgot,
And each long row began to grow
To fill the garden plot.

Gardens need fertilizer the same way people need vitamins. Our sheep have always provided us with some of the best: well-rotted manure. Chicken manure is too strong to make a good fertilizer, so although we raised a clutch of chickens in the days before high cholesterol warnings, we never used it on the gardens. Cow manure makes an excellent fertilizer, but our steers have never been kept in a confined space, so using their manure requires a walk through the pasture filling a bucket with cowflops.

For a few short years we had llamas, who have the tidy habit of picking a single spot to use as a bathroom. Even newborn llamas have this instinct. When Violet and Cuspidor had their first wawa (the name for a baby llama), Spitunia, within a few hours she had wobbled up to her parents' bathroom and happily added to the pile. Think of that - instant toilet training!

Few gardeners have access to llama manure, or even cow or sheep manure, but there are other ways to improve your soil. One of the best is to start a compost pile. Having a place for garden refuse means turning frost-blackened tomato and melon vines, dead marigolds and too-rampant evening primroses, gone-to-seed phlox and overgrown zucchini into rich, organic humus full of nutrients.

I never cease to be thrilled by the fact that all the green debris and wilting weeds I've dumped in my bins can turn into compost. It's on a par with having water turn into wine. Of course Mother Nature performs miracles like this all the time – lighting up the night with fireflies, painting rainbows in the sky, transforming a dismal swamp into a blaze of scarlet when the maple leaves turn each fall.

I always assumed that by incorporating such natural ingredients as compost and manure into my garden soil each year, I would be providing the ideal environment for plants. After all, Mother Nature knows best, and a successful vegetable garden ought to be adequate proof.

When scientists began learning more about chemical deficiencies and their effects on the human body, however, I decided that since all the vegetables we eat are raised right here on the hill, it would be smart to send a soil sample to the County Agent and get an analysis of its mineral content.

When I got back the results of the test, a three-page computer printout, I felt just the way I'd felt when the visiting nurse came to call a month after my first baby was born. That nurse showered me with criticism and unasked-for advice, starting with Trum's lack of booties and bonnet (on a warm July day) and ending with the suggestion that I might do well to give the baby a supplementary bottle in case I had insufficient milk. The fact that Trum was healthy and happy seemed completely immaterial.

The computer printout was as irritating as nurse Know-It-All, implying that Mother Nature and I didn't know best. It said my pH was too high and I should add 50 pounds of sulfur, plus 30 pounds of 10-6-4 to my 1500 square-foot garden. I don't believe in commercial fertilizers any more than I do supplementary bottles for nursing mothers. I ignored the Agriculture Department's recommendations and continued using my various organic fertilizers.

My first compost pile was nothing more than a continually growing heap of garden refuse up behind the barn next to the vegetable garden. When I remembered, I'd give it a forkful of manure, and eventually it turned into compost all by itself. Well, that's not quite true. Mother Nature's assistants, the earthworms, helped.

Tunneling their way through the pile, earthworms not only aerate the compost, preventing compaction and improving drainage, but also allowing excess CO_2 gas to escape. They make their tunnels in two ways. The hard way is to force a passage by squeezing particles of soil and debris closer together. The second way is probably not only easier, but also more fun, and that is to eat whatever's in the way. An earthworm's mouth is very small, but it can manage to take in all sorts of organic matter.

The food is first stored in the worm's crop, then ground up between fine grains of sand in its gizzard. Imagine that! Just like a chicken. A great deal of what is taken in is eventually cast out in the form of "wormcasts" – fine, well-digested droppings. Scientists calculate that the worms in an acre of sod will pass up to 36 tons of earth through their bodies in a year!

Most people can't make head or tail of an earthworm, but it has one or the other at either end. Charles Darwin, who took earthworms very seriously, could not only tell which end was which, but considered this lowly creature to be smarter than the ant. His experiments showed that a worm will always bother to seize a leaf by its pointed end, which makes it much easier to drag than if taken by the side or the broad end, while ants use brawn rather than brain when lugging home their treasures.

A worm moves by expanding and contracting the segments of its body and gripping the soil with two sets of bristles on each segment. When a mother robin starts pulling a worm out of the ground, the job turns into a tug of war as the worm grips the walls of its tunnel with its bristles and stretches itself like a rubber band.

Every earthworm is both male and female, but being companionable creatures, they work in pairs to fertilize each other's eggs. The babies are less than an eighth of an inch long and usually take two weeks to grow to full size.

Well, now that you know more than you need to about earthworms, let's get back to the compost bin.

When we moved the garden down to the backyard, the new compost bins were so close to the house that instead of a simple diet of weeds and garden leftovers, they began to get a taste of garbage goodies - eggshells, coffee grounds and orange peels - as well as vacuum dust, dead mice and the leftovers from Hank's haircuts.

Hank built the new bins into the side of the hill in the sheep pasture so I could dump compost into them from above and dig it out from below. That was a great idea, but did not allow enough air to circulate so the pile needed to be turned frequently, an exhausting job. The other flaw was that there were only two sections and they were almost always full.

Eventually Hank designed a new compost bin. Again it was built into the side of the hill, but it had no divisions and was wide enough to fit the new tractor's bucket, eliminating the backbreaking job of turning the pile. Periodically Hank scoops up a pile with the bucket and dumps it upside-down. It turns into compost twice as fast.

PACHYSANDRA

A pachysandra bed is as welcome to a lazy gardener as a toilet-trained two-year-old is to a lazy babysitter - no muss, no fuss. A well-established bed of this ground cover needs no trimming, clipping or weeding, and stays green all winter. What more could one ask? Admittedly it's a bit unimaginative, but so is a cup of coffee at breakfast. One can put up with that small drawback, especially if the bed has been planted as a buffer between grass and trees, stone walls or foundations that would normally require edging or hand-clipping.

Buying rooted cuttings instead of struggling with the long, tangled stems pulled from a friend's well-established bed is like buying a Stouffer's chicken tetrazzini dinner instead of making it from scratch. There's no question that nursery stock and Stouffer dinners make life a lot easier, but if you're as parsimonious as I am, you wouldn't dream of buying either. My recommendation, as you may have guessed, is to get your own bed started with free plants from a friend.

Find someone whose pachysandra has sprawled beyond its proper borders. My mother-in-law's beds, and those of half a dozen other folk of her generation, have invaded the woods behind or beside them. Find such a bed and you can just pull up handfuls of rooted pachysandra (assuming you have permission,) stuff them into a bucket of water and lug them home.

After you've prepared the soil, removing rocks and adding compost or leaf mold, you're ready to plant. Take some of those long, straggling stems from your bucket and trim away all dead and unhealthy pieces with a clipper. The stems are very strong and can't be broken easily by hand. When you can't find your clipper - mine is always disappearing in the debris - you can resort to biting off the parts you don't want, but it's a distasteful job as they have a very bitter flavor. If it's Spring, nip off all new top growth which will wilt with the trauma of the move and die of shock anyway.

The next step is a bit more finicky, but it's by far the best method for getting a full, thick bed in a short time. Dig a narrow trench about 4 inches deep along the length of the area to be planted. Lay the long stems in the bottom of the trench. Don't worry if they don't have many roots. Fill in around each leaf or group of leaves so they sit up straight. If there aren't many leaves growing on a single stem, lay several in the same stretch of trench. The next trench can be anywhere from 3 to 8 inches from the first, depending on your energy level and your supply of plants.

When the bed is fully planted, mulch it with oak or maple leaves or pine needles, tucking them around the greenery. Water the bed thoroughly. Then collapse in a deck chair and congratulate yourself. Within a year all those buried stems will have sprouted new growth and the bed will have turned into a thick carpet of green.

When I put in my first pachysandra bed using this trench method, my neighbor down the hill was putting in a bed with rooted cuttings he'd made over the winter by dipping them in rooting powder, then planting them in flats in his greenhouse. In the beginning, his bed looked like an orderly senior class, alert and attentive, and mine like a bunch of nursery-school kids. His was sparse and tidy, mine a hodgepodge of uneven green leaves.

Two years later my bed had become a lush and healthy ground cover, the buried stems filling in the gaps with new plants. My neighbor's was still tidy, and still sparse. He spent most of his weekends weeding it.

If you're contemplating pachysandra, look around the neighborhood. Someone's bound to have enough of this lazy man's ground cover to give you a start.

PERENNIAL PUPILS

I never wanted to be a teacher, but sometimes my garden flowers act just like a bunch of fifth graders. Each spring when school starts, they are all on their best behavior, arriving in class looking very neat and tidy. The bright blue clumps of Chinese forget-me-knots march down the border as if they were wearing uniforms. The daffodils look ready to have their pictures taken, and most of the other perennials are well-groomed and orderly.

As the school year progresses, however, one student after another begins giving me problems. There are always one or two failures who drop out halfway through the year, and a few real deadheads. There are also plenty of show-offs.

You might think Miss Peony would be my star pupil, but although she gets straight A's in almost all her subjects, she gets an F in deportment. If given the right seat (so the "eyes" are exactly two inches below the surface) at the right time of year (late September) peonies do their homework. They produce sweet-smelling blooms and handsome foliage, and rarely need individual attention.

Ah, but such posture! I've tried several ways of keeping my peonies upright, and find that laying chicken wire over the newly sprouting stems is the best method. The wire is invisible when the plants are full-grown. Even so, the blooms insist on leaning over to touch their toes after every rainstorm. My solution is to pick the open blossoms right away, floating these short-stemmed beauties in water.

The beauty queen of my class is the columbine. No one else in the border can compete with her long-spurred hairdo or her remarkable color combinations. Even when not in bloom, the columbine's dress of blue-green foliage is an attractive addition to the classroom. She's one of the first to arrive each year and requires no special help in class.

Delphiniums, on the other hand, do need extra help. Nothing looks more spectacular in the garden than the blue and deep purple spikes of these students, but if the teacher hasn't given them support early on, they'll fall flat on their faces during the first thunderstorm of the summer. Mine, even with special tutoring (winter protection), usually drop out in a few years. This year is a rare exception.

My best-behaved students are the obedience plants. They're so willing to face this way or that, always stand up straight and never demand special attention. The yarrows are equally well behaved and very brainy.

I guess the little feverfew could be considered the teacher's pet. She's so biddable, content to sit just about anywhere in the room, her sweet daisy-like blooms alert and attentive all through the school year. She always compliments her classmates, no matter what their shape or color.

I have lots of phlox in my class. They have trouble seeing me when they're all the same height, so I cut the front ones back in June so each clump resembles a choir in a raised auditorium. That allows all of them to see the conductor.

Teachers are always concerned about the deadheads in a class. I find Miss Iris the worst offender. Every single day one of her splendid fleurs-de-lis curls up into a brown unsightly spent bloom, detracting from those that follow. Lupines, too, become deadheads if not strictly disciplined.

Monarda, the shaggy red-headed beebalm, behaves quite well throughout the school year, but during vacation, she sprawls into other students' seats, stealing their notebooks, pencils, etc. She and artemesia have wrestling matches under the desks when I'm not looking.

I find the evening primroses are real bullies, staking out territory that rightfully belongs to other students. They can be kept in their place by a firm teacher with a sharp trowel, however, and their bright yellow flowers add lots of color to the classroom.

Then there are the late-bloomers, a whole family of asters, Alma Potschke in particular. She never contributes a thing all summer long, sitting quietly in the back row, but come September, she surprises everyone by turning into a real show-off, producing a giant display of brilliant pink blooms.

Being a teacher isn't an occupation I'd choose, but I guess I should be thankful. There's not one real cheater in my class.

THE RASPBERRY BED

Growing raspberries is about as tricky as growing a beard. I speak from second-hand experience, I hasten to add. Beginning a beard or a raspberry bed can be tedious, but once either is established, there is little maintenance except for a bit of pruning, and much pleasure.

Raspberry plants reproduce as rampantly as rabbits, so anyone with a well-established bed, even a parsimonious Yankee like myself, is usually happy to give away the small children that pop up in all directions each summer. These "suckers" come from underground stolons sent out by the parent plants, and will soon produce plenty of fruit.

Raspberry canes can also be ordered in the more orthodox manner - through the seed catalogs which offer the advantage of choice. Besides the old standbys such as Latham and Boyne, both hardy red types, there are many new ones with black or yellow fruit, as well as everbearers.

Whichever variety of raspberry you choose, don't despair when the plants arrive. They are sad little specimens with dried-up roots and single canes looking as dead as last year's Christmas tree. Soak them in a pail of water while you dig their holes. Once you've planted them, cut off the top half of each cane and give its roots a big drink of water from the pail.

Set the canes two feet apart in rows at least six feet apart. If you are planting more than one variety, keep ten feet or more between the beds. If you don't, the kids will sneak across to play with the neighbors each spring, and you'll never be able to tell them apart.

Raspberries are not in the least fussy about soil, provided it is well drained. They'll put up with clay or sand, a high pH or a low one. We mulch our beds each year with a foot-thick covering of old hay. This keeps down weeds as well as providing a nourishing organic environment. We also spread a pail or two of ashes from the wood stove through the bed each spring. Between the rows we lay strips of old carpeting from the Salvation Army store.

Once you understand the growth pattern of raspberry bushes, you'll find their pruning requirements quite simple. The plants are perennials, but their canes are biennials, living for only two years. The first year all they do is come up. The second year they branch, put out flowers, produce fruit, and, exhausted by all these heroic efforts, die.

In the fall when the first year canes are still green, the second-year canes look and are dead. Cut and remove them (most are brittle enough to break by hand at ground level), or you'll end up with a brier patch even Br'er Rabbit can't get through.

The first-year canes that remain - sometimes as many as ten to a plant - can be thinned down to the best five or six. These remaining canes should be cut back to two-thirds of their height, but this isn't essential. If you don't get around to it, Mother Nature will usually kill off the tops anyway.

Once you've pruned and mulched the bed and dragged away the dead canes, there's nothing left to do but look forward to another summer's bountiful harvest and the pleasure of picking and eating ripe raspberries for a month or more. Of course if you're one of those Puritan New Englanders who won't indulge in eating while picking, you will suffer mouth-watering agony as I do while you fill your basket, but I suspect there are few of us left. My children, although raised to be Puritans, have ignored my rule for years. They pick and eat at the same time and their baskets end up just as full as mine.

Whether you're a Puritan picker or a pleasure picker, the end result is a gastronomic delight - raspberries with cream, raspberry jam, and fresh frozen fruit all winter long.

DON'T LET POISON IVY GET YOUR GOAT

I suspect almost all families could tell a horror story or two about poison ivy – the brother who ate it, the mother who picked it to use in her first arrangement at the garden club, the son who had a terrible case in a vital spot during his honeymoon. My horror story took place when I was 12. I went off to summer camp, cried myself to sleep with homesickness the first night and woke up with my eyes glued shut with poison ivy. I spent the next several days in the infirmary. Not a good beginning.

Anyone who lives in the country or spends time communing with nature learns early on to recognize the three shiny leaves of poison ivy, and to keep a bottle of calamine lotion or its equivalent in the medicine chest. Can you remember that first blissful lathering of pink glop on the itching burning bubbles? Unfortunately I can also remember the flaking pink paint chips that soon dried up and made the itching worse than ever.

Poison ivy is a member of the sumac family and grows in most parts of the U.S. but does not grow in Europe. In spring the leaves have the color and sheen of mahogany veneer, but by summer the oval, pointed leaflets (only the middle one contains a stem) are a bright, smooth green, slightly hairy underneath. Mature plants have small greenish flowers in loose clusters followed by grayish round fruits.

The plant grows in a variety of ways. It can keep its stems underground and just send up short erect branches five or six inches high. Sometimes it sends long stems above ground that trail gracefully over rocks or scramble up and over fences. It can also take to the trees, its thick, hairy stems shimmying straight up a tree trunk. The hairs are actually aerial rootlets that help feed the plant.

We had all three varieties on Locust Hill when we moved here and spent years trying to get rid of them. Fortunately, both Hank and I seem to have built up an immunity to the taxocodentrol oil that causes the red rash and miserable itching, but there was always at least one of our daughters dotted with calamine like a circus clown.

In places where no other desirable vegetation grew, we sprayed the plants with kerosene. In other spots we uprooted and burned them, being careful to stay out of the smoke which contains enough toxic oil to produce a fiery case of poison ivy. There were other solutions, but in the end our answer was to buy a goat.

Goats have stomachs resembling cement mixers. Besides tin cans, nettles and cigarette butts, they will happily eat poison ivy. Comfort, a Nubian goat with long, velvet brown ears, was tethered each day in a new patch of poison ivy until the plants just couldn't take any more. As soon as all the ivy was gone, we put Comfort in the pasture with the sheep where she gamboled around in untethered freedom for a few days before discovering that the split-rail fence was a challenging "tightrope."

The morning I looked out to see her prancing along the top rail before leaping down into the perennial border to eat a few flowers, I decided she was no longer a comfort. Our ad in the paper offering a free goat located a new home for her, but not before she'd consumed most of the border. If you've got a crop of poison ivy you'd like to get rid of, get a goat, but only if you're willing to keep it on a tether and bring it water every day.

KEEPING UP WITH THE WEEDS

Are you the type of gardener who really wants to keep ahead of the weeds, but just can't seem to manage it? Here's a solution that works. Promise your spouse that if you don't weed the garden once a week all summer, you'll make a contribution to your least favorite charity.

Be it the Moral Majority or the Ku Klux Klan, the thought of sending even a few dollars to one you adamantly oppose is usually incentive enough to send you scurrying out to the garden. I happen to enjoy weeding, but I've used this method so as not to neglect my daily back exercises, and believe me, Teddy Kennedy hasn't gotten a nickel from me yet. And my back is getting better to boot.

Many of the most common weeds found in the garden are easily uprooted, and some are actually pretty good to eat. Purslane, known around here as Pussley, has fleshy red stems and is an interesting addition to salad, while the shapeless gray leaves of lamb's quarters make an adequate substitute for spinach and have twice as many vitamins. Even if you don't want to eat them, pull them. If you don't, they grow up to be pigweeds, annuals with a thick four-foot stem that will spill 100,000 seeds if not cut down in time.

The most difficult weeds are the perennials, as persistent as a whining mosquito at bedtime. The most ubiquitous one is the dandelion. It grows everywhere in the world. The dandelion's motto is "Never say die," as anyone who's tried to get rid of it knows. Dig as deep as you like with your shovel, loosen the soil, then pull slowly and with the utmost care, but I can guarantee you'll leave behind the last teeny bit of the root, and that's all a dandelion needs to produce another, or several new plants.

Certain cells called contractile cells growing in the meristem of a dandelion form this weak link, ensuring that a bit of root will be left behind if the plant is pulled up. The same sort of cells exist in the tail of a lizard. The lizard will grow a new tail, but the dandelion will grow a new head.

The parenchyma cells living just below the break are so versatile they can divide to form any sort of plant tissue - epidermis, xylem, phloem, etc. When they realize there is no longer a plant above their heads, they quickly produce dozens of new buds. The remaining tag end of the root also starts growing, and before you know it, a cluster of young plants has popped up in place of the one you got rid of.

The dandelion's shaggy flower is actually composed of as many as two hundred individual florets containing all the necessary parts to produce a seed. If each tiny parachute of sepals carrying a seed were to germinate, the earth, including the oceans, would be knee-deep in this hardy composite. Let's face it, we'll always have dandelions, so you might as well make use of them. You can use the leaves as greens, or in salads, the roots as a coffee substitute (not recommended) and the blossoms to make wine.

Everyone knows the definition of a weed - a plant growing where it is not wanted – a tomato in the rose garden, a rose in the vegetable garden. It's hard to think of a fancy tea rose as an undesirable plant even when it's growing among the peas and beans, but the rose known as a multiflora is another story. These roses happen to be the most destructive weeds on Locust Hill, creating impenetrable areas so full of thorny clawing branches that our dogs won't even venture into such a place to catch a rabbit. Yet one of my neighbors has a multiflora rose growing in the yard, a beautifully graceful specimen that fills the air with its heady perfume each June.

The reason multifloras have taken over half of Connecticut is because birds find their bright red berries a treat. As a consequence, they drop the plant's well-fertilized seeds far and wide. Drive from our corner of the state across to Rhode Island or down to the shore. Fields once open are now pure brier patches, taken over by multifloras.

The Agricultural Department was responsible for starting this plague. They recommended that multifloras be planted by farmers as a "living hedge" even a bull couldn't get through. It turned from a living hedge into a living hell, like so many other USDA recommendations – the kudzu vine, the water hyacinth. Admittedly multifloras are graceful and gloriously odiferous each June, but they soon become a menace, especially when they start to take over a pasture.

Another illustration of a plant that some might consider desirable while others would call it a wretched weed is the violet. These little flowers can be as hard to get rid of as dandelions. Prolific and promiscuous, they'll take pollen from the first bee to come along. They don't care where he's come from or where he's going. The result of such indiscriminate behavior is that new varieties of violets, known to botanists as "sports," are created.

A much more serious hazard is the fact that most violets are cleistogamous. That is not a description of an infectious disease. It merely means that besides the pretty blossoms nodding above the heart-shaped leaves of a violet, there's a second set of blossoms. These stunted greenish flowers have no petals and almost no stems. They are produced at the end of summer and lurk at the base of the plant.

These flowers look like buds or seed pods, and since they self-pollinate, they have no need to attract insects. As they ripen, each capsule turns brown and splits open, looking like three little canoes loaded with people. If you lift a clump of violets in late summer and shake it to get rid of excess dirt, all the people (seeds) get dumped out of their canoes. Unfortunately they don't drown, they just sink into the dirt and rise up again the following spring as new plants.

If you like violets, I suggest you buy them by the bouquet.

CORN ON THE COB

Like a lot of my generation, my first smoking experience was with corn silk. My cousin and I pulled out the dried-up brown threads from a few ears of corn, stuffed them into a corncob pipe and puffed and coughed, hidden under the branches of a bridal wreath bush in the back yard. That first smoke didn't taste very good, but it was certainly harmless compared to the weeds being smoked nowadays.

Do you know what corn silk's real purpose is? Each of those pale yellow strands is the style of a female flower. Within the immature husk, each filament is attached to an ovary that will grow into a kernel of corn when fertilized.

At the other end of each silk is the sticky stigma, waiting to catch a grain of pollen. Since there are about a thousand kernels on an ear of corn, there are also a thousand silks, which anyone who's husked corn well knows. The tassel at the tip of the cornstalk is the male flower, which is made up of hundreds of anthers, each producing about 2,500 grains of pollen.

The first summer we lived on Locust Hill, our new friends the Zinkes invited us to a corn roast – a culinary orgy of nothing but corn on the cob. Since childhood I'd been harboring a secret desire to just once eat corn until I could eat no more.

That night I succeeded. Between sips of bourbon and good conversation, I munched through one slow-roasted

66

ear after another. Imagine my embarrassment when at midnight I discovered my hostess had been counting. There was a tinge of awe in her voice as she informed me I had salted away a total of 26 ears!

We don't grow corn on Locust Hill. Instead, we swap our cow pastures and hayland in return for all the corn we can eat and freeze. Fresh frozen corn is the most ambrosial winter vegetable I can think of, and eventually I streamlined the job of freezing it so I didn't feel I should treat each package as if it were the crown jewels, brought to the dinner table only on state occasions.

Speed is the secret to sweet, melt-in-your-mouth winter corn - from plot to pot to Coldspot, as fast as possible. Good equipment makes everything go faster. A corn scraper is essential. I recommend Burpee's "Corn Cutter and Creamer". It first slits the kernels and then scrapes them off the cob. But even this stainless steel beauty is a useless piece of equipment without something to support it.

Hank made me a box with a lip at the bottom to overhang the kitchen counter, and a top that holds the cutter in place. The box is high enough so that a bowl can be slipped in the open side to catch the corn. This may sound complicated, but believe me, if you're trying to freeze 20 or 30 pints of corn without spending all day in a steamy kitchen it's worth it.

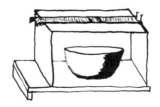

No blancher is big enough to hold full-sized ears of corn, so I use a large covered pot with a rack in the bottom, and steam my corn over 2 inches of boiling water. To facilitate putting the corn in and out, I use "cob-holders" made of hardware cloth, but you can easily make some out of bent coat hangers. They hold five ears, three on the bottom, two on top.

One more piece of equipment, not required but helpful, is an electric fan. Freezing corn is a hot job so if you haven't a fan, strip down to your underwear. Put a little Vivaldi or Handel's water music on the stereo.

If you've talked someone else into husking, like a thoughtful spouse or kids who want corn in January, you can start blanching when they're half way through, provided they're doing a good job eliminating the silk and the borers. Steam five ears for about five minutes. Then remove and cool (fill the sink with cold water and ice cubes), dry (folded dish towels next to the sink), cut (don't hurry this step or you'll end up with blood all over the corn), and stuff freezer bags (put back the bowl before you start cutting again).

Once you're into the rhythm, you'll find that all these steps combined take about the same five minutes as the steaming process. As you dump your five steamed ears in the sink, replace them with another five in the pot so this never-ending cycle never ends until all the corn is done. Eat the last five ears as a reward.

Ziplock bags are a big improvement over most freezer bags, but be sure to squeeze out all excess air. Lay the bags on cookie sheets and freeze them QUICKLY. If they're all sticking to the tray next day, give it a whack and they'll loosen right up. Then stack them tidily one on top of another for ambrosial winter eating.

IMPORTANT: Don't put off the job of cleaning up, no matter how tired you are. Corn turns to glue if left to its own devices. Washing tools, counters and floor right away will save a lot of agony.

FOLLOWING THE FASHIONS

I've never been one to follow the fashions, whether they be drinking wine spritzers, driving a sport utility vehicle or adding a deck to the house. Fads come and go as fast as a bowl of popcorn. Look at the hulahoop or that pathetic electronic pet that dies if you don't feed it.

Clothing fads are even sillier than toy fads. I can't imagine succumbing to the outrageous outfits designers design. Mini skirts, maxi skirts - let's face it, the only becoming length on most women is the one that hides the knees but doesn't look like a full-length gown cut too short. The colors fashion designers try and foist off on us are even worse. What's more unattractive than mauve or pea green?

Even when a new fashion is flattering, it takes me a year or two to adapt. I guess that's why I buy all my clothes in the thrift stores where everything is nicely out of date.

It seems hard to believe, but gardens follow fashion just like clothes and toys. How absurd! Here's a description of a fashionable garden designed in 1912 by Beatrix Farrand. "...the epitome of elegance and restraint. Clear forms, spare ornaments, the academic formality of the plan, and the use of constructed narrative (here linking man and nature,) evoke European precedents but transcend pastiche."

If I wrote such pretentious stuff I suspect my readers would disappear as fast as the eclairs Hank buys for me on rare occasions.

Following garden fashion in the 1600's meant rigid formalized lines of sculpted hedges and geometric patterns. "Rooms" were created, bounded by clipped yews or high walls. By the 1700s such geometry had become unfashionable. Gardens began to blend with the broader landscape. Rolling land, ponds, clumps and belts of trees became the trend, and flowerbeds were considered too man-made and artificial to fit into such natural landscapes.

The cottage garden, the rock garden, the island bed, the color coordinated border in pure white - all types of plantings have come and gone and come again. And of course the flowers themselves have also had their ups and downs. Ten years ago the plain pink and wine-red hollyhocks that stood beside the barn in farmyards were scornfully discarded as old-fashioned, and replaced by fancy double-ruffled varieties. Now they're right back in style.

I don't follow flower fashions any more than I do other fashions, but I read an article recently in *The Wall Street Journal* of all places, discussing just what will be labeled trendy or tacky this year. It's the nurseries that set, or try to set, the fashion in flowers each spring, and according to the nursery owners interviewed for the *WSJ* article, the big cry this year is annuals.

Annuals add "more color, more sophistication and bloom for a longer time in the summer." Sophistication?? The nurseries are trumpeting annuals for their "drama and variety," and poo-pooing perennials with their limited bloom time. They don't mention the fact that annuals must be re-purchased every year.

Nurseries (there are over 12,000 independent retail outlets in the U.S.) do about $3 billion in sales of flowers and garden equipment each year. Obviously selling you a peony that will last for twenty years isn't quite as profitable as selling you six or seven flats of annuals every year. And not just simple varieties like petunias and pansies - they're considered only suitable for tract housing - fancy hybrid varieties are what the nurseries are recommending this year.

Frankly, I find all this hilarious. Do we really care what is fashionable in the world of garden design? Can flowers really be tacky or sophisticated or transcend pastiche? I grow whatever appeals to me, and think you should do the same.

STAKING TOMATOES

How tomatoes like hot weather! Mine have grown beyond their stakes. Tomato vines with poor posture end up in mud and slug territory, so any gardener worth her fertilizer provides good support for them.

There are as many ways to hold up tomato plants as there are to hold up a woman's stockings. The elastic garter (which must have been great for circulation!) was the first method we ladies used to keep our stockings up. Then along came the garter belt. Believe it or not, Hank's great-grandfather invented that funny little clip and the Thomas P. Taylor Company manufactured the very first garter belts in Bridgeport back in the 1890's.

When I was a kid, the lady who came every Thursday to iron our sheets and shirts had another method for holding up her hose. While she worked, Mrs. Majeska had her stockings rolled down around her ankles like doughnuts, but before waddling out to catch the bus at the end of the day, she'd sit on the back steps and roll them up, stretch the tops in her fat fingers and twist them into an ingenious knot.

Stocking supports have practically become obsolete with the creation of panty hose, but no one's come up with anything to eliminate the need for tomato supports. The old-fashioned way to support tomato plants is by tying their stems at intervals to wooden stakes - hockey sticks, bed slats, sawed-off sumacs. Provided they're strong and tall enough to pound deeply into the ground, stakes are a fine way to help vines form good posture habits.

What to use for ties depends on what's around. The box labeled "String too short to use" won't do, but if you've got that kind of attic, you may well have a box labeled "Stockings too bad to save" which will. Stockings are soft and elastic, but I have to admit they look unseamly.

The one problem with tying up tomato plants is that you can't get the job done once and forget it. You must add more ties as the plants grow. That's good though - it gets you out there snipping off the suckers that seem to sprout overnight in the crotch of each branch. If they aren't removed, they'll take food needed for the ripening fruit.

Far easier than tying your vines at intervals, is to attach a long piece of string (we use baling twine) to the top of each stake, and then tie the other end around the base of the vine. As the vine grows, just twist the string around it every once in a while. Works like a charm.

If your garden is enclosed by a fence you can eliminate the need for stakes by planting your tomato vines next to it. Since tomatoes are happier when given a different spot in the garden each year, don't keep them on the same section of fence every summer. Wire cages are another way to support your plants and using them allows you to move your plants into the garden early if you've wrapped the cages in clear plastic.

The need to support tomato vines may be tedious, but we girls should be thankful the need for stocking supports has been eliminated by pantyhose.

IT'S TIME TO DIVIDE THE IRIS

When the last fleur-de-lis on your irises curl up and turn brown, it's time to think about dividing the plants. If you do this job by early July they'll have plenty of time to re-establish their roots before winter. If you do the job too close to cold weather, the first September frost will heave them out of the ground.

Irises don't need dividing every year. It takes about three years for plants to grow enough to get overcrowded, but whether it's people or plants, overcrowding is an invitation to disease. In the case of the knobby knuckles of iris plants, the disease is root rot, which looks and smells as bad as gangrene. I've never actually seen gangrene, much less smelled it, but you probably haven't either, and I bet we both have an equally repulsive mental picture of it.

Get out your spading fork and loosen each clump of iris and lift it carefully, gently shaking the dirt from the anchoring roots. Break the rhizomes apart, discarding old or diseased-looking ones. If any are slimy with root rot, disinfect the soil where they lived with formaldehyde or bichloride of mercury. Prune the healthy rhizomes so none is longer than three inches. Cut the leaves back in a fan shape. (This should be done even if plants are not being moved.) Let the plants sit in the sun so their cuts can heal over while you're fertilizing their new bed with bone meal.

To replant the rhizomes, make two slanted holes in the soil, side-by-side, and set the rhizome on the ridge between them as if it were riding a horse. Tuck its anchoring roots down on either side and cover them firmly with soil. An iris adds new growth at only one end of its rhizome, so plant them in a half-circle with their fans facing out from the center. That way it will take them longer to crowd each other.

Iris is most effective planted in clumps of a single color, but if you're given rhizomes by a gardening friend who's been dividing and multiplying, you will have a problem on your hands. With all the telltale blossoms gone there'll be no way to tell blue from yellow from white unless your friend has been thoughtful enough to mark them.

I have a very generous but slightly bird-brained sister-in-law who brought me 30 iris plants one summer.

"They're the most heavenly colors," she gushed.

It was obvious, however, that the mystery of which rhizome would produce which color would remain a mystery until the following June. Since single iris plants look even sillier than multicolored clumps, I planted groups of three or four together. The following spring my garden was a riot of color. I don't really like riots, but it seemed like a lot of work to dig up plants that didn't need dividing, so I lived with them in all their motley glory.

The year I faced dividing them I tied a piece of appropriately colored yarn around the stem of each one in preparation for the big move. I dug them all up in July, divided them, cut their leaves into fans and set them in piles. I had seven piles of seven different colors. At least I did when I went inside for lunch. When I came out an hour later there were iris rhizomes scattered across the lawn in all directions, and Rosta, our incorrigible water spaniel, was prancing around tossing rhizomes into the air with delight.

After screaming at the dog for a while, I shut her in the trash shed and began sorting again. By some miracle the colored yarns were still on most of the plants. I planted them carefully in single-color clumps in the border, murmuring apologies for the terrible treatment they'd received, and stuck the unknowns up behind the barn.

The job took most of the afternoon, and I had long forgotten the incorrigible Rosta by then. A few demanding barks from the trash shed around suppertime reminded me. I was amazed that she hadn't complained earlier, but as soon as I let her out I saw why – she'd been tossing around trash all afternoon.

A MATCH MADE IN HEAVEN

A few years ago when granddaughter Brittany was just a toddler, I let her out of my sight one day and the next thing I knew she was way up in the sheep pasture with her arms around the ram. Fortunately he was a young and unaggressive one, and although he did back off and butt poor Brit before I could reach her, no serious harm was done.

That night Hank and I decided we'd have no more rams on Locust Hill. If we wanted to continue having baby lambs, we'd buy them. So the next April I started looking in the classifieds for new lambs. When I found the following ad I couldn't quite believe my luck.

"Will swap sheep or lambs for plant material — trees, shrubs, perennials. Call…"

What an ideal barter for the bargain hunter of Low Cost Hill! I called, said I was looking for three lambs and what would the lady like in return.

"I have a backyard full of mud," was the reply. "I'll take anything you're offering."

That weekend, Daffodil, a sweet, white-faced lamb out of a picture book, and Daniel, a jet black baby boy arrived in a pick-up truck, along with dozens of empty flats and flower pots. In return the lady went home with ivy and pachysandra, evening primrose, phlox, forget-me-nots, lobelias, feverfew, and lemon lilies. At last my border had some space for new plants.

The second day the lady brought her husband. They dug up popples, locusts, maples and clumps of white birch from the woods. I'm afraid it was pretty stony digging, as the husband looked exhausted and cranky by the time he'd loaded their truck with all those saplings, but his wife was grinning from ear to ear.

The third day the lady came with Dilly, a browny-black girl lamb. She went home with some laurel and four or five barberry bushes from the sheep pasture.

Barberry bushes? I'd never thought about it before, but actually barberry bushes are attractive shrubs, provided they're not taking over your pasture. They have inconspicuous yellow blossoms in spring, but turn a colorful red in the fall and have bright red berries that are considered good food by a variety of birds.

The lady had also dug up a young multiflora rose bush. It looked sweet and gentle, but I explained that it would grow up to be a thorny monster and would strangle everything nearby, and furthermore, its seeds would be spread all over her neighborhood by the birds. It took a while, but I finally convinced her to leave it behind.

I've made quite a few swaps in my day. I've done other people's taxes in return for a bushel of peaches. I've paid the yard boy in giant pumpkins and swapped raspberries for a ham (when you have your own beef and lamb, there's nothing so good as a ham...) None was as satisfying as the swap of plants for lambs.

GLADIOLUS

Gardeners face up to the death of their vegetable and flower gardens each November without too much trauma, knowing that come spring, lush green life will be reborn. The grim reaper who takes away friends is not so easy to face. In the past four months Hank and I have lost almost a dozen elderly friends and relations, seven of them male, four female, a typical ratio I'm afraid.

The only good thing to come out of all those funerals was that we sat down and wrote out the instructions for our own funerals. We picked out our favorite hymns and psalms, and named which charities we'd prefer "in lieu of flowers." Hank chose Ducks Unlimited, with Planned Parenthood as an alternate for those who didn't approve of duck hunting. I opted for the Northwest Hospice. We both preferred cremation to wasting space in the good earth.

This all may seem macabre, but I think it's nice to have a guideline of one's spouse's preferences, whether you follow it or not. Hank's eccentric great-uncle wanted a cocktail party instead of a funeral, and requested that he be stuffed and propped up in a corner with a glass in his hand. We have a friend who wants everyone to sing "Old Black Joe" at his funeral. My aunt had only one strong desire about hers - NO GLADIOLUS!

Lots of people associate these fancy bulbs with the last rites of passage and heartily dislike their rich spikes of color for just that reason. I have no such hang-ups, although I undoubtedly never would have grown gladiola bulbs had Yung's Nursery not offered half a dozen free each year with my seed order.

The first year they arrived I was in a quandary about where to plant them, since no clue to their colors was included in the bag. I ended up by putting all six in the perennial border. I was astonished at their size and how well they looked set among other blossoms.

Since the decorating colors in our house lean toward rust-red, pumpkin and green, at the end of the summer when I dug up the bulbs, the three that had been on the pink and purple side I put in a box to be replanted in the border, while the white, yellow, and a treasured soft orange I put in a separate box to be planted in the cutting garden the following year.

Provided only the blossom is cut for bouquets,   the leaves will allow the bulb to store food for the next year's bloom. After I'd received free bulbs from Yung's for four or five years, sorting each batch in a similar fashion, I had a large supply that complemented the border, and another equally large pile to cut for arrangements.

Now don't put your nose up at the idea of an arrangement using gladiolus. All alone I admit they aren't my style   any more   than   the name "glads" - an abbreviation as tacky as "drapes."   Mixed with other flowers, however, such as zinnias, snapdragons and a bit of baby's breath, they complement any bouquet.

If you grow gladiolus, you already know how to treat them, but for the benefit of those who have scorned them in the past and are now looking with a less jaundiced eye, here's the scoop. The bulbs should be lifted with a fork before the first hard frost and set out to dry (not in the sun) for several days. Then the old corms, shrunken from giving birth to those fat spears of summer bloom,   are broken off and discarded, the new ones that have formed stored in a cool dry place where they won't freeze.

Think about trying a few of these showy bulbs next year. There are miniature varieties if you feel that large ones are too ostentatious.   And think about what sort of funeral arrangements you'd like as well.   Better too soon than too late. Who knows, maybe your spouse would hire the Tanglewood chorus to perform Brahms Requiem at your funeral.

BITTERSWEET,
AS CONTROVERSIAL AS ITS NAME

If roses are for Valentine's Day, lilies for Easter and poinsettias for Christmas, bittersweet is for Thanksgiving. Unlike most holiday decorations, bittersweet doesn't cost a penny. Just drive along a back country road in November and you'll have no trouble spotting this vine twining its stems over shrubs and tree branches and sporting clusters of attractive red berries in orange caps.

Few people who have bittersweet growing on their land begrudge someone clipping off a few branches. I'm embarrassed to admit it, but I once was one of the few. When we lived in Fairfield we had just one bittersweet vine growing on our property. It was down by the road and I planned to use it to decorate the Thanksgiving table.

In mid-November I was heading down to the mailbox when I heard a car door slam and a female voice cry, "There's some, Millie!"

Realizing someone was about to take my Thanksgiving decoration, I hid behind a tree and announced in a deep authoritative voice, "THAT BITTERSWEET IS ON PRIVATE PROPERTY."

The culprits froze, then scuttled back to their car and drove away. Since I am now just like those ladies – forever cutting or digging up Mother Nature's offerings - I cringe as I think back on that day.

I doubt if many other people are so stingy they'd deny you a lousy bit of bittersweet, but you may not like the idea of snitching your Thanksgiving berries from the roadside. Don't, however, decide to grow your own bittersweet, at least not in your yard. I made that mistake. In all of Locust Hill's acres I'd never spotted any bittersweet, so I dug up one from my sister-in-law's woods and planted it beside the ugly propane tank, thinking it would hide the tank as well as provide me with Thanksgiving decorations.

That vine grew faster than the mold on stale bread, but it never produced any berries. Eventually I discovered the reason why. Bittersweet vines are like humans, they're either male or female, and if you don't have both, you're not going to get any berries. The female vine may blush and bloom each spring, but if there isn't a male flower around to provide her with pollen, it won't do her a bit of good.

By studying the blossoms on my vine with a magnifying glass as if I were Sherlock Holmes, I learned they were boys, not girls. By that time, the vine had gone berserk, burying not only the propane tank but tearing up the fence behind it, running wild in the sheep pasture and climbing the walls of the animal barn until he had managed to get in the window. What sort of sex-starved monster had I brought into my yard anyway?

I decided to replace the bittersweet with a vine that had better manners. That summer I cut the stems down to the ground and painted the stumps with brush killer, but by September the roots had sent up new sprouts. I'm not talking about a few weak stems. I'm talking about a twenty-legged octopus waving tentacles in every direction. It took another two years of poison to finally kill it.

I recommend you find your Thanksgiving bittersweet along a back country road. DON'T make my mistake and plant some in your back yard.

DECIDUOUS VS. EVERGREEN

It seems ironic that the first tree we planted on Locust Hill was one to replace the only decent-sized tree on the place, a tall Norway spruce. By then we'd put a large dormer window in the attic-like room we'd chosen to use as the master bedroom, and realized that this giant evergreen was blocking all winter sun from the room, but was in the wrong place to block any summer sun.

Trees are cheap if you are willing to dig up a small sapling from the woods and have a lot of patience. Hank has a great deal of patience. He wanted to plant an oak! Since my patience is limited, I preferred a popple, the fastest growing tree I could think of. "That's a trash tree," Hank argued. "It will blow over in the first high wind."

We ended up with a silver maple, another fast grower Hank put in the "trash" category. We found a young one only five feet high, root-pruned it in April and transplanted it in May. Digging a proper hole among the roots of the spruce took an ax and a lopper, but we managed. But asking our young transplant to live beneath the shade of a giant Norway spruce and surrounded by a jungle gym of roots, was like expecting a juvenile to thrive in reform school. I knew it would need coddling if it was to survive.

Around the corner was a fantastic example of a pampered tree, the sugar maple. It lived directly over the primitive septic system we had inherited. Thrilled with the bounty supplied by a family of five, it grew by leaps and bounds in the first few years we inhabited the farm. By the time we could afford to put in a real septic tank, it had reached the same height as the Norway spruce.

I began feeding the new silver sapling the next best thing - sheep manure mixed with hay, plus plenty of water, an essential for newly planted trees. Each year we sawed off a few more of the lower limbs of the spruce to provide it with light. In three years it was almost twelve feet tall and had gotten a crick in its trunk trying to reach the sunlight beyond the spruce. It was time to cut down the sun stealer.

It may seem a sin to cut down a thirty-year-old tree in the prime of life, but to me it's just like killing a beautiful coyote who's been eating your sheep. We felt no hesitation about slaughtering the spruce. Our hesitation came in deciding where to make the first cut so the tree wouldn't fall on the house. The alternative to destroying the house was to have the tree fall toward the pond, so we waited, Hank patiently, me impatiently, for winter to turn the pond to ice.

On a sunny afternoon in January, Hank finally got out the chain saw. Our giant evergreen crashed onto the ice exactly where it was supposed to, but from then on things went from bad to worse to catastrophe. As Hank began sawing limbs off the felled tree and the children and I began dragging them into a pile on the ice, the sky turned leaden. Soon we felt the first drops of rain and within minutes we were soaked. We retreated to the house. By nightfall the rain was a steady downpour and the ice was groaning against the pain of a January thaw.

The spruce took its revenge. By the time the rain had stopped two days later, it had sunk to the bottom of the pond. As cold returned, the ice formed once more, locking spruce boughs in its grip. It looked as if we'd planted a dozen little evergreens in the middle of our pond. It remained that way until mid-summer when we finally managed to drag the trunk out onto the lawn and cut it up.

The silver maple, despite being labeled a trash tree, is still with us. It lets sun warm the bedroom each winter and provides much-needed shade in summer. The Baltimore orioles always choose one of its swaying branches in which to build their pendulous nest. Each spring I have a perfect view from the bedroom of this project as well as the first flight of the babies.

CHRISTMAS TRADITIONS

Most families have their Christmas traditions, carried on faithfully from one generation to the next. We have one you've probably never heard of and another practiced all over the world. The first is called "The Broom and the Basket." A stout laundry basket and a very stout broom are needed to play this game. Both were readily available in my grandmother's day, but are sometimes hard to find now.

The broom is slipped through the handles of the basket and its ends rest on the seats of two straight-backed chairs so that the basket rocks freely about a foot above the floor. Four handkerchiefs are draped over the corners of the chair backs and the "victim" sits on the broom handle, his feet in the basket, steadying his precarious position with a cane.

The object is to knock each hanky to the floor with the cane without falling out of the basket. How we loved this ridiculous game when we were kids! Not only playing it, but watching our elders play. Seeing proper Uncle Louie grimacing through his walrus mustache as he straddled the broom, or our white-haired grandmother in her long skirt and pointy-toed shoes aristocratically wielding her silver-headed cane was a marvelous sight. But now that I'm a grandmother myself I'm not so crazy about falling out of the basket, the fate of most players.

The other tradition, kissing under the mistletoe, I feel just the opposite about. As a child I avoided this game, disliking my knock-kneed boy cousins and my bristly-bearded uncles, but the older I get, the more I enjoy being caught under the mistletoe.

Mistletoe has been around for centuries, but it wasn't until the 1700's that the quaint idea of kissing under it came into being. At first the custom included removing one of the pearly white berries after being kissed. Once the berries were all gone, it was considered very bad luck to be kissed under it. This limited the amount of kissing, and consequently this part of the custom was soon dropped.

Mistletoe is an evergreen, producing small yellowish blossoms in February or March. It doesn't grow in New England, but can be found in our florist shops at Christmastime. I have a friend in Natchez, Mississippi who sends me a bunch in her Christmas package each year, wrapped in feathery gray sprays of Spanish moss. Both of these parasites grow on the live oaks in her yard and are considered a terrible nuisance. The bushy clumps of mistletoe are very long-lived, dying only when they've managed to kill their host tree.

The Latin name, *Phoradendron viscum,* unattractive as it sounds, is a good description. *Phoradendron* means tree thief, while *viscum* describes the mucous-like quality of the berries. When a bird eats a mistletoe berry, he ends up with a very sticky beak. He cleans it by wiping off the viscous pulp, to which a few seeds usually adhere, on the side of a branch.

The pulp hardens to protect the seed until germination, at which point a sucker root penetrates the bark of the tree and connects with the vascular tissues. Sounds a bit like Dracula, doesn't it? Forget all this when you hang up your sprig of mistletoe and just enjoy a little smooching. It's not half as dangerous as playing "The Broom and the Basket."

SPRING CHORES IN THE BORDER

I think spending three days shoveling out the sheep barn would be bliss compared to doing taxes. This year's Schedule D was a nightmare. Because of the change from 28% to 20% for capital gains, a full-page worksheet was provided. It was so awful that when I finished it I found Hank and read him the entire page: Subtract line 35 from line 34, Multiply line 36 by 10%, Enter the smaller of line 19 or 27, one mind-boggling instruction after another. When I finished reading, Hank got up and crossed the room, knelt down and kissed my feet. What a great guy!

I've read that more than 50% of citizens in the *lowest* tax bracket use an accountant. There really should be a law requiring the President and the entire Congress to do their own income taxes unaided. Any one of them caught getting assistance, along with the accountant who assisted, would be fined $100,000 each. I know, I know. Congress would never pass such a law, but I suspect we'd get a simplified 1040 in a hurry if they did.

Thank you. I feel better! When something infuriates you, it really helps to bellyache a little, doesn't it? After I mailed both state and federal taxes, my blood pressure was still boiling, so I went out to work off some steam in the garden. I usually start my spring cleaning with the ivy beds, but I chose instead to work in the perennial border and had a marvelous time grabbing bunches of dead stalks and viciously breaking them off at ground level.

Most gardeners I know clean up their flower beds in the fall. That's when I always did it until the year Hank and I took a September vacation to visit English gardens. We survived a head-on collision (driving on the right side of the road is the wrong side in England), but I was still too crippled to do any garden clean-up when we got home.

The following spring I discovered the dead stalks of perennials that have been through the long winter are dry and brittle and twice as easy to get rid of. Instead of cutting down each individual stem with a clipper, you can grab an entire handful, rock it back and forth once or twice and break off an entire clump at once.

Most stalks - phlox, aster, heliopsis, astilbe - all break off easily. The two exceptions, at least in my garden, are peonies and gooseneck loosestrife, *Lysimachia clethroides*, which has gracefully arching spikes of tightly-packed flowers. Both these perennials have such stringy stems that even after a long winter they require clipping.

Admittedly, looking out at a lot of dead stalks poking up through the snow all winter isn't too attractive, so if you're a tidy gardener who likes to keep her gardens pristine, this idea may not appeal to you. On the other hand, if you're like me (the type who puts off housework until we've invited guests for the weekend) you'll find the ease of spring cleaning worth putting up with the winter's untidiness.

After I'd tidied up the border I decided to edge it. It was only recently that I learned how to properly edge a flower bed. I've always been too stingy, never leaving enough room for the lawn mower's wheel to ride inside the bed without squashing dozens of plants and chopping off the heads of a dozen others. When I let the wheel ride right *on* the edge it always mushed the edge down so the grass had an easy time creeping into the bed.

No garden book seems willing to describe the proper way to edge a flower bed, but last spring I saw some beautiful beds that had just been edged by a professional. They had close to a three-inch deep cut at the edge with the bed's soil banked up to be level with the lawn so the mower would cut the grass well. The plants had been arranged so that none would be run over by the lawn mower.

I went home and re-edged my 100-foot border that way. I have to admit there are times it doesn't pay to be a cheapskate. Now if I could just face paying an accountant to do the Taylor taxes!

INSIDIOUS INSECTS

When I first started to raise vegetables, I was totally unaware of how distressing it could be to have the garden invaded by insects. An army of aphids, a slime of slugs, a camouflage of cabbage loopers - the devastation caused by insects makes the gardener as frustrated as a dog with fleas.

The first time my garden soil hatched a collection of cutworms I had no idea what it was that had toppled four out of eight young broccoli seedlings in a single night. I tugged gently at the first wilted plant in the row and found it had been completely severed from its roots.

Horrors! I rushed down the hill to my farm neighbor, who had a huge and healthy vegetable garden, for enlightenment. "Aw, you got cutworms," she told me scornfully, as if anyone should have known. "Pesky durn critters. Just take some old tin cans from the trash and cut the bottoms out, then sink 'em round the plants when you set 'em out. That'll do the trick."

Well, I don't know about your trash, but mine's pretty disgusting. I fished around in the smelly barrels, taken to the town dump only once a month, and came up with some repulsive old soup cans, washed off the mold and sank them around my replacement seedlings. Sure enough, they did the trick, but the next year I learned a much easier method for outsmarting Mr. Cutworm.

This vicious grub has a "modus operandi" similar to that of the Boston Strangler. By day he stays hidden, but at night he crawls around in search of a victim. When he finds one, he must curl completely around it to do any damage. This means he can be totally stymied by two or three long nails pushed into the soil around the stems of young plants.

The mother of the cut worm is the innocent little miller moth fluttering under the porch light on warm September evenings. Mrs. Miller likes nothing better than soft, friable garden soil in which to lay her eggs, and that fact guarantees trouble for the gardener the following summer. There's no way to keep Mrs. Miller out of the garden, but the nails, or even toothpicks, make good weapons against her offspring.

All too many harmless looking moths, flies and butterflies give birth to garden enemies. The cabbage looper's mother is a little beige moth whose white eggs hatch into microscopic loopers. They grow fat and happy eating the leaves of all the *Brassicas*. The worst thing about loopers is cooking them along with your broccoli by mistake. They turn a virulent-looking yellow. Of course if they didn't, you'd probably end up *eating* them by mistake.

The small gray fly who lays her eggs on the leaves of spinach and Swiss chard dooms these two vegetables to a maze of leaf miners, tiny maggots that tunnel inside the leaves, turning them brown and dry. The only solution is to cover the plants with cheesecloth. The first crop of spinach in spring is usually safe, however, as the mothers of leaf miners don't start laying their eggs until late May.

The eggs of a black and gray-striped fly half the size of a house fly turn into the writhing of root maggots that attack cabbages and cauliflower underground, their secret devastation unnoticed until the young seedlings suddenly turn yellow and wilt. Putting collars of tarpaper around plant stems deters the mother of these headless maggots from choosing to lay her eggs in the garden.

The sphinx moth, who does most of her flying at twilight, sipping nectar from deep-throated flowers in the manner of a hummingbird, is responsible for the eggs that hatch on the underside of tomato leaves. The larvae, as green as the leaves they will feed on, are no bigger than inchworms, but the more they eat the more grotesque they become. The resulting four-inch-long monster is the tomato hornworm, his anal horn sharp as a needle, his sides decorated in white diagonal stripes edged in black, and his minute front legs a squiggling bristle just below the mouth.

The first time I detached one of these repulsive creatures from a tomato plant and squished it under my sneaker was a shuddering but necessary ordeal. If I'd left him to continue gobbling up tomato leaves, he would also pupate, continuing the life cycle. The hard-shelled pupa would live in the ground through the winter and turn into a new sphinx moth the following spring.

Fortunately the hornworm has another enemy besides the gardener, the braconid wasp. She not only stings this great green caterpillar, but deposits a number of eggs just beneath his skin. The eggs hatch into young grubs that feed on the fatty tissues of the hornworm. As adults they emerge from beneath the skin and proceed to weave themselves into little white cocoons that stand on end all over the hornworm's back.

The sight of a great green hornworm crawling on a tomato stem is bad enough, but one stubbled with white-wrapped baby wasps is really disgusting. Even so, you should leave these hornworms alone, as tiny new wasps will soon burst from the cocoons, eager to carry on their life cycle, laying their eggs in the bodies of other hornworms.

Wet summers bring another hazard to the garden, a slime of slugs, especially if you use mulch. The word *mulch* comes from the German *molsch,* meaning soft and rotten. That may sound like two-day-old garbage, but it doesn't have to be *that* unattractive to keep the soil moist and friable. Because we always store more than enough hay bales to feed the sheep and the burro all winter, I used to use left-over hay to mulch some of my vegetables.

Unlike many mulches, hay decomposes rapidly and adds nutriments to the soil. The bales split into tidy blocks so I can lay them like tiles on a bathroom floor, close together and at least four inches thick. Unfortunately in a wet summer, they are an open invitation to slugs.

The slug's method of travel is about as charming as a kid with a runny nose. To get from place to place he slides over his own mucus. For this reason, he prefers his road to have a smooth surface. Sprinkling cinders around the base of plants will discourage him, but a bucket's worth of cinders is about as easy to find as a carpet beater.

In the rainy summer of 1982 I discovered my mulched garden was not a garden at all, but a vast holiday hotel for slugs. All the conveniences – good food and comfortable beds, moist and dark and perfectly suited to slugs. They arrived in droves, like slippery politicians gathering for a national convention. The continuing rains guaranteed that the rooms would be booked to capacity all summer.

I'd never had trouble with slugs in past summers except to flick one or two off the lettuce leaves. Just harmless, shell-less snails, right? Wrong! When they arrive in the collective noun form they can turn your lettuce and broccoli leaves and ripe tomatoes into Swiss cheese before you know it. And since they sleep all day and only start carousing after the sun sets, it may take weeks to figure out who they are.

Ruth Stout's solution - putting out saucers of beer each night, edges level with the soil, and collecting dead or dead drunk slugs the next morning is too expensive for this old skinflint, and since it's the yeast in the beer that attracts the slugs, I mix yeast and water in my saucers instead, a cheaper solution that works just as well.

PREPARING FOR A WEDDING

Over the years my perennial border grew without rhyme or reason as I divided and multiplied and gratefully accepted second-hand plants from friends. It wasn't until I began preparing for the first Taylor wedding in 1980 that I thought about revamping it. Trum, the bride to be, wanted to be married in the garden, and gave me this information a year in advance so I'd have an entire summer in which to perfect the border.

By then the border stretched along the full length of the sheep pasture's split-rail fence, close to 100 feet. Since the wedding ceremony would take place right there in front of it, I decided I should change its characterless straight edge to a scalloped one. I'd edged the original border with bricks, but after a few winters of frost heaves they disintegrated.

Bricks are impractical in New England, but I didn't think much of the corrugated edging sold by nurseries, be it plastic or metal. After much thought, I decided I wouldn't have any divider. I would merely make a clean sharp edge between the border and the lawn with the edger.

Since the border is backed by the split-rail fence, it was easy to measure the scallops. They would curve out from two feet to five feet and back again between every other fence post. I put in stakes at the proper intervals and looped the hose from one to the next so I'd have a smooth line to follow as I cut the scallops.

Then we (Trum worked as hard as I did) tackled the hard part. Since the original border had been 3 feet wide, we could dig up and move sections of lawn from where the bed would increase to a five foot width and use them to fill in the places where it would narrow down to the two foot width. It was an exhausting job and took us almost a week.

Ah, but then came the fun part – rearranging the perennials. Lupines, iris and peonies were to be the main attractions, all guaranteed to be in bloom for a June wedding. Besides a scattering of feverfew and artemesia, we planned to add some annuals at the front of the bed the following spring - snapdragons, petunias, sweet alyssum.

Each time we lifted and transplanted something, we also removed rocks, some as big as basketballs, and added compost. Not wanting to move any perennials while they were still in bloom, it took most of the summer to complete the new arrangement, but it was worth it.

On the wedding day the sun beamed down, the border bloomed with color, and as the ceremony began, the sheep, curious to see what all the people were doing out there on the lawn, came down to their side of the fence, their bells accompanying Elgar's Pomp and Circumstance (playing on the sauna's speaker).

All three daughters had their wedding receptions on Locust Hill. All three wore my wedding gown, (with gussets added, removed, and added again,) had a homemade zucchini wedding cake and convinced the sun to shine all afternoon.

In other respects, the receptions were very different. Bridget, our middle daughter, chose to be married in May when little was in bloom but daffodils and Chinese forget-me-nots. Tam, our youngest, chose September when an entirely different set of perennials were blooming in the border.

Even so, the thought of having a hundred or more wedding guests perusing the property was in each case as affective as a cattle prod. I often think it would be nice to have one more daughter who could choose to be married in the winter so I'd be inspired to fix up the inside of the house instead of the outside.

EINE KLEINE NACHTMUSIK

Sit on the front porch on a summer evening and listen to the night noises. Mellow or metallic, sweet or shrill, melodic or tuneless – the air is filled with sound. Unlike good children who are seen but not heard, these creatures are usually heard but not seen.

It all begins with the sweet piping of the spring peepers. As the soft gray pussy willows turn to yellow catkins and the last hepaticas bloom in the woods, the volume of this cheerful chorus grows deafening. Everyone knows the peeper's song, but few have ever seen the singers. The tiny frogs that make up this mighty chorus are less than an inch in size when full grown, but their song travels almost a mile.

The proper name for the peeper is *Hyla crucifer*, a reference to the small black cross on his brown back. Like all frogs, peepers pop out of their eggs as tadpoles, so small they can hardly be seen with the naked eye.

Before the swamp turns green with the accordion leaves of wild hellebore and the round fat foliage of the skunk cabbage, the peepers' gills and tails have magically turned into lungs and feet. Freed from their watery beginnings, the little frogs hurriedly hop the long journey from swamp to woodland where they'll spend the summer eating insects.

As April slips into May and the wooly fiddleheads of the cinnamon ferns uncurl, another choir composed of courting tree frogs tunes up each evening. Tree frogs are not much bigger than peepers. They live in the treetops all summer and are amazing arboreal acrobats. They are able to leap from one branch to another with ease because of the large disks on their fingers and toes.

True to their name, *H. versicolor,* tree frogs can be brown, gray, green or mottled. By July the leafy branches of maple, ash and oak are alive with their music, an enthusiastic trilling as contented as a cat's purr. One night a few summers ago the chorus of tree frog trills in our front yard was so stupendous that I went out to look. Apparently dozens of tadpoles had simultaneously metamorphosed into tree frogs. Hopping up the bank from the pond, they'd mistaken our daughter's bicycle for a tree. The handlebars and seat were solid tiny green frogs, squished together and trilling with all their might.

As summer grows apace and fields fill up with tangles of purple vetch and the snowflakes of Queen Anne's lace, we begin to hear a new, far harsher song, the rasp of the katydid. The great green katydid is a long-horned grasshopper who makes his summer noise by scraping the toothed file on his left wing with the "scraper" on his right wing. Normally he "picks" his tuneless banjo only twice, "katy," but sometimes three times, "katydid." He's likely to repeat one or the other at least 30,000,000 times a summer.

Along with the discordant clamor of the katydid, another familiar sound reaches the ear, for the pond frogs, both the green and the leopard, have grown large enough to start their evening croaking. These guys (females hardly ever sing) squat in the shallows, their heads just out of water, their throat sacs white and wrinkled beneath their chinless faces until they puff them up like balloons to croak.

Along with the cacophony of the croakers there are usually a few deep chuggarums as the grandfathers who've lived through the winter clear their throats. We had a large bullfrog population in our pond that faithfully gave their predictions of rain on summer evenings.

I said *had* because a few years ago we got a new dog, a Benji-type mutt, who quickly discovered that frogs were as entertaining as wind-up dolls. Each summer Hidie spends hours catching them, carrying them gently onto the lawn and releasing them. Unfortunately, like most mechanical toys, the poor frogs eventually run down and no longer work. Although Hidie probably hasn't totally decimated the frog population, she seems to have gotten all the grandfathers as we rarely hear chuggarums any more.

Another summer sound that fills the air when days grow sultry with August heat is the scratchy buzz of the cicadas, constant and monotonous. All the cicadas, from the 17-year variety that remains underground for that length of time, to the annual, dog-day cicada that is the primary food of the digger wasp, emerge from the soil to live for only a few brief weeks. Then they retreat to lay their eggs and die.

During August they live in the treetops, enjoying the hot weather and making their atonal buzzing both day and night. The noise they make is created by vibrating a pair of membranes with the muscles of the abdomen.

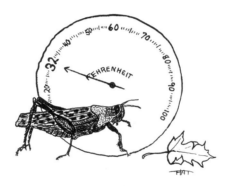

The finale of the summer's symphony is produced by the cricket. As the days grow shorter and green turns to gold, this shy black instrumentalist suddenly appears on the front porch or even in a corner of the living room, tunes up his squeaky violin and offers us a plaintive requiem. Many authors have described the cricket's song, but I think Hawthorne said it best: "If moonlight could be heard, it would sound like that, an audible stillness."

When the little black cricket's sweet notes can no longer be heard, Autumn has buried Summer under a blanket of fallen leaves and the only sound remaining is the sigh of the gardener as she puts away her trowel.

I never wanted to grow strawberries, having read that they were good for only two years and the first year's blossoms had to be removed to ensure a bountiful harvest in the second. I can see leaving asparagus alone for the first year to enable its roots to become well established. After all, that one year will be followed by a lifetime of picking asparagus. With strawberries, all the work of planting, mulching, picking off blossoms and runners, etc. would be done for a single year's crop? No way.

I decided to grow strawberries purely for decoration the summer of our oldest daughter's wedding. The fall before Trum got engaged we'd faced the fact that the sills at the back of the house, buried underground and encased in cement, must be replaced. Removing at least 2 feet of soil from the backyard was a necessity if the new sills weren't to follow the path of the old ones, but it was a major job.

Gas, oil, water and electric lines leading to various outbuildings crisscrossed the area. You'd think we were tearing up a city street! Fortunately Elihu, who is a very talented backhoe operator, managed to nudge out every one and then re-lay it another foot deeper. Once the new sills were in and the area smoothed over, we were left with an ugly cut of raw earth around the perimeter.

Obviously some sort of retaining wall was needed. And soon. The thought of a hundred wedding guests viewing the mess we'd created in the backyard was worse than the possible cost of putting in a retaining wall. Fortunately making a wall of old railroad ties turned out to be not only the quickest solution but the cheapest; Hank got permission to take some old ties from along the tracks in town that had recently been replaced.

The nine-foot long ties had been rolled down into a swamp beside the tracks and were thirstily soaking up the stagnant water. Rassling one up to the track was worse than wrestling an ornery bull calf out of a mucky stall. Each tie seemed heavier and more filthy than the last. The one we put on our grain scale weighed in at 210! Loading ten ties on the handcart someone had kindly left on the tracks, we'd then push them (unfortunately uphill) up the line to the cattle truck we'd borrowed and winch them in.

Luckily Trum and Clem, her husband-to-be, were as eager to get Locust Hill presentable for the wedding as we were. While Hank and Clem lugged ties into place, interweaving them at the corners, Trum and I nailed them together with 12-inch spikes. In a single weekend we'd built the wall and a wide staircase leading up to the driveway.

Hank claimed the backyard looked a lot like Fort Apache, especially the section that was five ties high, so I decided to plant an edging of strawberries at the bottom and top of the wall in hopes it would soften its forbidding look, and might even provide a few ripe berries to put in our champagne on the wedding day.

I ordered seventy-five plants the next spring, planted them along the wall and mulched them with pine needles, which supposedly enhances their flavor. Since I was growing them purely as decoration, I removed no blossoms, and although no berries were ripe on the wedding day, there were plenty by the following week.

Because the beds were backed by the wall of railroad ties, runners had nowhere to go but into the lawn where they were easily snipped off by the lawnmower. The best news, however, was that the following year and the year after that and in fact even three years later, we were still picking enough berries to make jam as well as enjoying strawberry shortcake and berries on our cereal.

The berries got smaller and smaller, but they tasted just as good as big ones. Each year I did a bit of transplanting of runners, replacing plants that looked tired. It wasn't until the eighth summer that berry production had completely dried up and I ordered another 75 plants.

TURN YOUR BEETS INTO WINE

Tiny, tender beets are just delicious fresh from the garden and their leaves come close to spinach as a green, but when they get to be the size of tennis balls, they're not so tasty. It's easy to ignore this root vegetable when summer squash and fresh beans start coming along. When tomatoes and corn are finally edible, who would think of having beets?

For many years I pulled my unused beets and threw them on the compost pile, a painful solution for a parsimonious penny pincher, but then one Christmas I was given a pocketbook titled "How to Grow Wine in your Own Kitchen," by Mettja C. Roate. It had recipes for elderberry wine, dandelion wine, and every other wild ingredient you can think of, but there were also many that called for common vegetables such as carrots and beets.

That summer I harvested 23 pounds of purple tennis balls, eager to convert them into wine.

While I washed the beets with the hose and cut off their tops and tails (no peeling necessary), Hank got out the cider press so we could put them through the grinder. The bucket of mush that resulted was a glorious royal purple. I cooked it with only six quarts of water, and after straining it through cheesecloth, we had so much juice we had to rummage around in the top of the long shed to find enough crocks to hold it all.

We added 12 pounds of sugar and a whole jar of wheat germ, not to mention a heaping tablespoon of peppercorns, and ended up with four big crocks sitting on the table in the playroom. Before long the whole house smelled like a brewery. The kids stirred the liquid each day, intrigued by the fizz and bubble and hiss.

At the end of two weeks we strained all the wine through a nylon stocking, returning it to the crocks to "settle" for two days, then bottled it in quart soda bottles with screw tops. We'd heard enough stories about home-made wine blowing up in the cellar that we were super careful not to tighten down the tops till all the bubbles had disappeared.

Ms. Roate recommended not using this particular wine for a good six months, but naturally we had to at least *try* it. It had been sitting in the cellar less than a week when we opened the first bottle. Wow! Firewater! Was it the peppercorns? It was as hot and strong as cheap brandy.

I can't remember how many bottles we'd filled - a dozen or more - but we'd tried at least two more by the time the six-month deadline rolled around, each smoother and less eye-watering than the last. The ones opened after February were amazing. I'm no wine connoisseur, but I remember Hank sipping and saying, "That's as good as a good Madeira, m' dear."

I'd love to end on that line, but unfortunately I must be honest and tell all. The following year we again made beet wine - 40 pounds worth. What a waste of sugar! It was undrinkable. We were never sure why, but I suspect it was the beet crop. Beets are quite like people - some grow sweeter as they age, others turn bitter. That year's crop was probably on a par with the choleric teacher I had in fifth grade.

HIRING THE YARD KID

The days of cheap help on Low Cost Hill vanished when the kids stopped living at home, and I'm afraid they won't return until the grandchildren get old enough to help the old folks with chores. In the meantime we've learned to cope with the hired hand. We prefer 13 to 15-year-olds who, once trained, will still be around for a few years.

If you're planning to hire help this summer and don't know any promising youngsters, ask your postmaster or the 8th grade teacher in the local school. They usually know who's available. If not, walk your dog around the neighborhood in the early morning and chat with the kids waiting for the school bus. Pick kids who look bright-eyed and bushy-tailed rather than those who appear sullen or half asleep. There's no guarantee they won't reverse personalities by afternoon, but in talking to them you'll get a feel for which are reliable, hard working and on the ball.

Over the years we've hired kids to roof roofs, pick up hay, dig trenches, garden and mow lawns. We even paid one to catch fish the year our pond shrank to such a mud puddle that we had to remove the amurs, our weed-eating fish, to more liquid quarter. We've learned from our mistakes – and theirs – what makes a good yard kid.

Few youngsters like to ask questions for fear of sounding stupid. Telling them to ask helps, but it's best to spell things out carefully and thoroughly before turning them loose on a job. We learned this lesson the hard way.

One day Hank asked the current yard boy to put gas in the tractor. Later, when he started up the tractor, Hank still heard gas sloshing emptily in the tank. He unscrewed the gas cap and peered in, then asked Jimmy, who fortunately hadn't left, whether he'd filled it.

"Oh, yes," Jimmy replied eagerly, "but I put the gas in the *other* tank," and pointed to the radiator!

Don't assume a job is easy just because you're been doing it for 20 years. Handling a shovel, an iron rake or even a wheelbarrow takes experience. The first-time shoveler has no idea how important the thigh muscle or the foot is in helping put leverage against a hard pile of dirt. Teaching your helper to shovel properly is not only a kindness, but will get the job done in less time.

Don't assume your helper has a perfect memory. Expecting him to mow so that cut grass is throw *away* from the flower beds by telling him/her just once probably won't be sufficient, and you'll be pulling sprouted grass from the beds all summer. When you're explaining a job to a novice, tell a few tales about your own stupidity – in other words, laugh at yourself so your helper will feel less nervous about making errors. Even the brightest kids can make mistakes.

One summer we hired a capable 17-year-old to help with the haying. Hank cut the first two swaths, involving difficult edges, showed Bruce how to raise and lower the cutter bar and turned the job over to him. The one hazard left was fairly conspicuous – a single telephone pole near the middle of the field. I don't know which girl Bruce was dreaming about, but he managed to wrap the cutter bar right around that one pole!

Don't forget the compliments. Criticizing a bad or sloppy job is certainly in order, but should be offset by plenty of praise for the good jobs. You may have mulched the garden in only an hour in past years, but you should still compliment a kid's two-hour job, unless you looked out and saw him lounging on a hay bale for twenty minutes.

Good yard kids are like good drivers, they anticipate. They don't fill the front of the trench before filling the back. They shut gates, put away tools and don't stand around waiting to be told what to do next. The best ones like their jobs and take pride in how they do them. You may go through three or four before you find a good one, but it's worth the search.

CARPATHIAN WALNUTS

In 1972, ten years after moving to Locust Hill, we planted our first store-bought tree, a Carpathian Walnut. This tree has nuts almost identical to English walnuts, but because it originated in the Carpathian Mountains of Eastern Europe it can tolerate the freezing temperatures that we in the Icebox of Connecticut, along with our trees, learn to survive each winter.

Getting the nut tree was Hank's idea. He ordered it from a catalog. When it arrived, he eagerly removed its protective wrappings and proudly held up an anorexic twig without a single leaf to hide behind.

"By the time that thing produces nuts enough for a Waldorf salad, you'll be gumming it," I laughed.

But Hank had the last laugh. The Carpathian grew fast. Soon it looked just like the lollipop trees children draw in kindergarten, a fat circle of greenery atop a short but sturdy trunk. Ours is now thirty feet tall. Its leaves are large and provide dense shade in summer, but they're anything but attractive when fall arrives. They turn an ugly brown, looking as if some mechanic's oily rags had escaped from the clothesline.

We planted our Carpathian at the edge of the front meadow and mow under it so the nuts will be easy to find. We didn't have to mow for the first 6 years, but finally one May we were thrilled to spy blossoms. Hank rushed to get out the lawn mower and waved the recipe for Waldorf salad in my face, but there were no nuts come fall.

Discouraged, we got out the tree book and learned that not until its second year of bloom will there be both male and female blossoms and a harvest of nuts. From then on we could expect a good crop every other year, a slim one on the off years.

When a walnut ripens properly it falls out of its husk to the ground. If there's a high wind or rain at the wrong time it may be blown off the tree with its husk still intact. When that happens, the husk must be pulled off, an unpleasantly slimy task, but necessary if the nuts are to dry out. Fresh off the tree, the nuts are too moist to eat. They should be stored in a dry place for a month or more. When we can't wait, we zap a few in the microwave.

Nut trees don't need spraying and are generally healthy. Squirrels are their main enemy. One of our neighbors has an unusual solution to outfox the squirrels. Some of his tales are taller than trees, however, and should be taken with a grain of salt. He claims he has made four or five boxes, each with a hinged bottom and a squirrel hole on the side. He hangs the boxes in his nut trees each fall so the squirrels can use them to store nuts in for the winter. When the nut-gathering season is over, our neighbor goes out with a basket, unhooks the hinged bottom of each box and collects the nuts.

Squirrels never get our walnut crop as our dogs are good squirrel catchers and our tree sits in an open meadow. Our problem is that with a bushel or more of nuts each year, we end up making brownies once a week and put on a lot of unneeded pounds. I guess we should be making Waldorf salad instead.

THOSE NOTORIOUS CALF HUTCHES

Calf hutches, lined up in rows on dairy farms, are a familiar sight in our area, but few people know the first thing about them. I'd like to set the record straight.

Before calf hutches were invented, newborn stock was kept in the barn, usually tethered in a dark corner with little ventilation. Bacterial diseases spread fast in such close quarters, so if one calf got sick, so did all her friends. Drafts and sudden fluctuations in temperature caused respiratory infections. Despite plenty of disinfectant and antibiotics, the calf mortality rate was high.

No one worried about the problem, however, except the farmers. People driving by a dairy farm couldn't see calves that were tethered in the barn so they assumed they were romping around in some pretty meadow, happily nurtured by their own mothers, a practice that vanished years and years ago. Now that calf boxes are lined up conspicuously along the roadside, everyone's upset about "inhumane conditions."

A calf hutch may look small as seen from a passing car, but it is no little box. A mouse living in an ice chest would feel more crowded. A calf enclosure is over seven feet long and more than three feet wide. It is deep enough to protect the calf from summer sun and winter wind and is kept as clean as a doghouse. It has a large open doorway facing south, a window facing north and a ridge vent in the roof.

As soon as a newborn calf has received that first vital nursing of colostrum from its mother, it is given ear tags and taken to its new home, usually a hutch with a large fence around its entrance. The hutch has been steam-cleaned since its last occupant, lined with fresh straw and moved to a new position. If I were a calf I'd find my box pure bliss compared to being tethered in the fetid darkness of a barn.

Newborns are bottle fed twice a day with whole milk

for about ten days. They are then tethered to a hutch without a fence and fed grain and milk supplement for the next three months. Next they're sent to school, put with other youngsters in big airy pens so they can learn about sharing, competition and getting along with others.

Talk to any farmer and you soon realize that calves are "the babies" of the family, treated not only with care but with affection. Hutches usually are lined up somewhere between the farmhouse and the barn so anyone passing by can stop and say "Hi." The calves, provided with fresh air, sunlight, and a little green grass to nibble, stay clean and dry and above all, healthy.

The calf hutch idea was dreamed up by Wisconsin farmers and proved to be such a success in reducing calf mortality that it quickly was taken up by New England dairy farmers. Unfortunately rumors that the "poor little fellows" in the hutches were being fattened for veal became so common, that even our local residents believed them.

THE CALVES LIVING IN HUTCHES ARE NOT BEING RAISED FOR VEAL. These calves are all baby girls. They will grow up to be heifers, and once bred, will become milk cows. All boy calves are taken to auction before they're a week old. Most are bought by farmers who raise veal. No Connecticut farmers raise veal.

Boy calves raised for veal (mostly in Pennsylvania) are kept indoors in a controlled temperature of 60 - 65 degrees. They're fed no herbaceous food, only milk and special grain, which results in the pale, iron-deficient meat. They are kept on this diet for about a year before going to slaughter. You are entitled to feel sorry for them only if you never buy veal or order Veal Marsala or Veal Piccata when dining out in a restaurant.

Next time you pass a dairy farm, stop and let your children pet some of the babies. These future milk cows will even eagerly suck your fingers. Don't feel sorry for them. They are both happy and healthy.

Farming methods have changed about as much in my lifetime as marriages have. I can still picture the local farmer and his sons who mowed our family's meadows when I was a kid, pitching loose hay atop a horse-drawn wagon. I can also recall a lot of couples who pitched in and made their marriages work right up until "death us do part."

Well, times change, and although I'm partial to the old-fashioned ways, I sure would hate to be haying with nothing but a scythe and a pitchfork. Our hayfields produce a first cutting of over 2000 bales. Even with modern methods, Hank and I don't try to cope with more than the 350 in the front meadow, letting a local farmer handle the rest.

Haying is a three-day process and you just have to hope Mother Nature's on your side when you start to cut. Venerable, the 1939 International Harvester tractor we inherited with the farm, is enormous. When I climb up onto its rusted iron seat I feel like a king sitting high up on the palace wall with my kingdom stretched out below me.

The lot we mow is not what you'd call choice. Parts of it are so steep you feel as tilted as a windmill as you round the corners. The first step, cutting it (usually Hank's job) is a very logical process. Once the morning dew has vanished, you start. When you come to a corner you lift the hydraulic cutter bar, make a loop and drop the bar as you head down the next swath. Provided you get the end of the bar in the grass-free line of the previous cut, all goes well, but the bar is a good 8 feet long so you must watch carefully.

If no little raindrops dampen the next 24 hours, the cut hay will be cured enough to rake. Raking the field (my job) is not logical at all, for if you rake in the same pattern that you've cut in, you'll end up unable to rake the middle of the field without ruining the previously raked windrows.

The rake sticks out from the tractor, preventing anything but broad sweeping turns. Square corners will never do. You must bow in on the long stretches and dip out at the corners so you can continue to have room to turn. This means raking hardly any windrow on the turns, just little wisps of hay tipped out of the rake. It took me years to understand the theory behind this crazy-looking mess and I would end up tied in knots in the middle of the field, unable to avoid goofing one windrow after another as I tried to make impossibly tight corners.

The next step, baling, we've always left to a pro, preferring not to rent or borrow this delicate piece of equipment. Most balers ka-thunk, ka-thunk the hay until it is packed to the right size, then automatically tie two pieces of twine around it and dump it onto the ground. One year the farmer baling our hay had a broken twine tier, so his wife sat on the back of the baler tying twine as fast as she could. Every once in a while we'd hear a pleading voice wafting up from the meadow, "Slowwwer, Walter, slowwwwer!"

A hay bale weighs anywhere from 30 to 60 pounds. After you've hoisted a few they seem to weigh about 100, but there's a marvelous camaraderie when everyone helps lug and load the truck. Sometimes thunder rumbles in the hills, prodding us to greater effort, but the sun has lost its fierceness and draws long cool shadows across the stubble, giving us that little extra bit of energy to finish.

At last the barn is filled with pastel green, tightly packed blocks of hay. Our bodies ache and our legs and arms sting with sweat and scratches, but the smell of newly mown hay is heady, and so is the feeling of a job well done. The menagerie of animals on Locust Hill once more will have plenty of hay come winter, and Mother Nature didn't spoil a single bale.

Nowadays more and more farmers grow corn instead of hay. One of the farmers that rented the hayfields on Locust Hill asked permission to plant corn in the Longlot, a 15 acre meadow stretching north and south between the house and the cow pasture. The corn fields in the valley, whispering in the wind, are a beautiful sight, but we soon realized it's quite another story if they've been planted in your own backyard.

We all know that corn gets as high as an elephant's eye. What we hadn't realized was how hemmed in we'd feel when those endless corn rows were all we could see. How we missed watching the heifers in their pasture, the occasional fox or coyote trotting by on the way to the waterhole, the rare sight, back then, of a wild turkey. With no sweet meadow grass and clover to browse, seeing deer at dusk vanished as well.

How we longed for the soft sweep of meadow to walk through instead of the rasping, sharp-edged leaves of the corn stalks slapping our faces when we needed to cross the Longlot. Our whole family waited eagerly for summer's end when the big machine would come and shear the corn stalks, grind them up and spit out the results into the chuck wagon following behind like an obedient puppy dog. At last we could see once more across the field.

But what was left behind was a bleak and bony landscape of stubble, occasionally blackened with funereal crows, snatching up the meager kernels of leftover corn. Neither the thinly seeded rye planted in late October nor the sketchy snows that followed succeeded in hiding the raw earth and broken corn stalks.

The following year we found a farmer willing to turn the Longlot back into a meadow.

We have a lot of fences on Locust Hill - woven wire fences that enclose the two sheep pastures, barbed wire ones for the two cow pastures, and a fence around the vegetable garden. When you have that many fences, you need a method to get over, under or through them, and we have a nice variety.

Our cow pastures have what we call "Texas gates," a sloppy method of making a gate. It's just a continuation of the barbed-wire fence, its end post slipped through loops at top and bottom of the gate post. It's awkward and difficult to shut as the barbs get tangled together and its poles sag. I learned recently that in Texas this type of gate is called a Yankee gate, in Maine a Canuck gate, in Bavaria a Prussian gate. Obviously no one wants to take credit for it.

One of our barbed wire fences stretches between our house and daughter Bridget's cottage on the other side of the meadow. It contains no gate of any sort, having been put in long before there was a need for one. For the first few years after Bridget and John built their little house, we crawled under this fence every time we went over there, all too often catching our rumps on a barb.

Eventually we found the perfect rock, beautifully flat and about 1 and 1/2 feet high and moved it just halfway under the first strand of barbed wire as a stile. Step up on one side, swing a leg over the top strand of barb and step down on the other side. Since grabbing hold of the wire could be nasty, Hank slit pieces of black plastic tubing and slipped them over the wires to make a pleasant handhold.

The gate to the vegetable garden is the one I really want to tell you about. We call it a No-wait Gate and I wish Hank would patent it, but patenting inventions is a complicated business, so feel free to build this gate for your own vegetable garden. I probably go through this gate twenty times a day. Consequently Hank designed it so that I can open it with ease even when both my hands are occupied. Whether I'm balancing a grandchild on my hip, carrying buckets of compost or pulling the garden cart, I open and shut this gate with my foot.

The No-Wait Gate consists of a light wooden frame four and a half feet wide and three feet high. It has a diagonal support and is covered in light wire. Simple 2" hinges hold the gate 3" above the ground. The edge of the gate opposite the hinged edge rests on a notched piece of wood, rounded on the end. This "catch" is nailed at ground level perpendicularly against the gate post.

Because the hinge pins of the gate have been replaced by finishing nails of a smaller diameter, they provide enough "give" to allow me to lift the gate up and over the notch with my foot to open it, or slide it over the rounded end to slip back into the notch when closing the gate. Look, Ma, no hands!

Neither our dogs, our burro nor our sheep can figure out how to open the No Wait Gate, and our grandchildren learned to lift it with their hands at about the same time that they learned how important is to SHUT THE GATE! They delight in slamming it. It is wide enough to handle a garden cart or wheelbarrow, even a carefully led burro.

The gate leading from the vegetable garden to the sheep pasture and the compost pile is made of boards and has spring hinges so it shuts by itself, letting the rounded wooden hook attached to the post slip down over the top edge of the gate. I longed to have a "no hands" sort of gate there, as I almost always have my hands full when using it.

This year I figured it out. I tied a piece of nylon string to the back of the hook and attached it to a board the size of a foot pedal, its back end resting on the ground, its front two inches off the ground. I step on the pedal and the hook rises, allowing me to open the gate. Look Ma, no hands!

THE LLAMA DRAMA

Yesterday Hank and I moved Cuspidor, the life-size wooden llama daughter Bridget made me a few years ago, planting him in front of the ugly new satellite dish. He looks great, but he sure ain't the real thing. I don't know any domesticated animal with more appeal than a llama. The pair we bought back in the early '70s was more fun than a circus full of clowns.

Nowadays llamas go for several thousand dollars, but we paid a mere $200.00 for Cuspidor and Violet, half for the beasts themselves, the other half for the animal trainer and his two helpers who loaded them in our friend Rob Mead's truck. Fearing we'd be charged another hundred for unloading the pair when we got to Locust Hill, we decided to do that end of the job ourselves.

We didn't know much about llamas back then, but we'd already learned one thing in a hurry. When llamas are upset they spit. Spit is a very polite word for the rancid regurgitated glop they can shoot 20 feet or more. Since Violet was such a placid female, we'd had little trouble herding her into the truck, but Cuspidor worked up quite a few furious spitballs before he was forced to join her.

By the time we reached home, an incredible odor filled the air, so potent even Henny, the kids and I, sitting fifty feet away to watch the unloading, wrinkled our noses in disgust. Violet and Cuspidor, their necks entwined like a push-me-pull-you, were huddled in a corner of the truck, their ears laid back, their eyes wide with fear or fury, we weren't sure which.

That afternoon was one of the funniest we've ever spent. Once the truck was backed up to the pasture gate and the tailgate let down, we'd assumed the llamas would eagerly march down the ramp to their new home.

How naive we were!

An hour later they were still ensconced in the truck. There is no coaxing or prodding an angry llama, at least not if you want to keep your clothes clean and not end up redolent of a sewer. Even though Hank and Rob were holding the children's sliding saucers for protection, these shields were not sufficient to protect them from the slimy missiles being spit with such deadly accuracy. If they shielded their faces, the llamas sprayed their pants. If they moved the saucers down to save their clothes, their faces became targets.

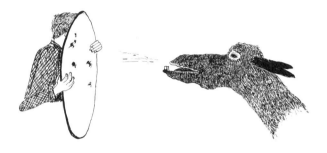

Rob finally suggested they tilt the truck bed and dump the silly buck-toothed beasts on the ground, but that also proved a failure. The steeper the angle, the further back into the truck the llamas retreated, managing this man-made mountain with ease. Next the men tried using a 4x8 sheet of plywood. It protected them from attack while they eased it behind the two stubborn animals and forced them to the very edge of the ramp.

There they remained. Neither Hank nor Rob wanted to give the final shove for fear of breaking one of those matchstick thin legs. Exhausted, as much from laughter as from their wasted efforts, they decided to take a break. Their audience, Henny, the kids and I, our sides aching with two hours of constant laughing, also needed a break.

As we all headed for the house, we heard another sort of laugh, a llama laugh. We looked around just in time to see Cus leap gracefully over the ramp and land a good six feet beyond it where he arched his long neck and let out another great whinny. Violet daintily stepped down the ramp behind him.

That day was only the beginning of the llama drama. Through three years and three wawas (baby llamas,) Spittunia, Expectorius and Hawk, we enjoyed the antics of these very special pets. Cuspidor would spend hours making amorous overtures to Violet, but when she was pregnant she always kept him at bay, twisting around to spit as he chased her. Soon after each birth, however, she'd relent and we'd hear a loud and contented humming from the pair as they spent a romantic afternoon together.

Sad to say, the llama drama ended with tragedy. We'd acquired our pets before anyone discovered the cause of the sudden paralysis that crippled both mother, father and all three wawas. Had they eaten poison sumac, water hemlock? When we called the Catskill Game Farm for information, they confessed that they'd had over twenty of their herd fall ill with the same trouble. All were autopsied, but the mystery remained.

It was only a few months after our last llama died that scientists discovered that fresh water snails carried the disease. Llama farms now inoculate their herds against it, but the news came too late for ours. My wooden llama is a poor substitute for the graceful creatures who brought us so many laughs. I'm afraid he doesn't compare. He doesn't turn his ears into question marks or rear up with whinnying laughter, eat cigarette butts or spaghetti, or even pasture grass. He looks much too stiff. I think I'll buy a clematis vine to plant next to him.

THE GREAT RUBBER POND

The pond on Locust Hill was a leaky failure for over twenty years. The County Agent had warned us, but we'd stubbornly ignored his advice. At first having a dried-up mud hole in the front yard didn't matter much since the rest of the yard was equally unsightly. But as we eliminated falling-down fences and outbuildings, built terraces and landscaped, such a prominent eyesore became truly painful.

We'd eliminated the weeds with the amurs, and because of the sauna, were able to swim when the pond was full, but our efforts to solve the leaks had all proved fruitless. Our first attempt, dumping bags of Bentonite clay in the pond to stop the leaks, was a waste of money. Next we laid a pipe line from the pond all the way to the upper well, thinking an additional supply of water would help, but it barely made a dent – the tide continued to go out.

Since the sheep pasture was always soggy, we decided to see if a dowser could find water there. Wow, how that dowser's stick dipped! I do believe in dowsing, but frankly I don't know why after that experience. The dowser found four places he claimed had major veins of water just below the surface. Not one produced water when we dug them.

We might still be living with that eyesore of a pond had I not taken a bookkeeping job for a man who made industrial sludge ponds for chemical companies. Learning that these ponds were lined with heavy industrial roofing rubber, I quizzed my new employer on the subject.

When I heard the musical words, "I can get it for you wholesale," I quickly convinced Hank that we should finally do something about the ugly crater ruining the landscape on Locust Hill. The fact that each of us had just come into a sizable inheritance made the idea conceivable.

Ironically, the first step was to drain the pond, full of water from several weeks of September rain. Then we had to dynamite the immovable boulder at the center of the pond. This dramatic operation, done by a professional, revealed the biggest reason the water level of the pond had gone up and down like a yo-yo. A vein of water lay beneath the rock, helping to fill the pond when the ground water level rose, but sucking water out when it was down.

During the first week of construction the amount of equipment surrounding the pond reminded me of a clutch of bright yellow insects feeding on a bit of food - bulldozers, backhoes, trucks, a crane, a cement mixer. It was a monumental project, but mainly because we'd decided to have a retaining wall built on one side that tapered from nine feet down to four feet to increase the pond's depth.

We watched, fascinated, as the pond's shape changed. The water was diverted into a trench, the foundation and the retaining wall poured, pipes for drainage and overflow set. Then it was our turn to get to work - picking up any stone bigger than a plum pit and spreading two inches worth of dead sand over the entire area so all would be smooth when we put down the rubber.

On the day we rolled out the first 10x100 foot roll of rubber, we'd gathered a total of 14 friends and relations to help. It was a very sexist afternoon. The girls were given the job of scrubbing talc off the rubber with some sort of horrible acid that burned and quickly ate through our cheap rubber gloves. It was a far worse job than scrubbing floors. Then we painted a wide strip of contact glue to either side of each overlapping seam, trying not to breathe the fumes.

When the glue ceased to be sticky to the touch, anywhere between five minutes to half an hour, depending on the temperature, the macho men came along, pressed the overlaps together and rolled the seams with a steel roller. I hate to admit it, but we girls didn't have enough strength to do this job properly, and doing it properly was essential. We managed to finish four rolls of rubber that first day and covered almost half the pond.

On the second day quite a few helpers were missing, in fact the original 14 had been reduced to 9. Who could blame them? It was so hot in that black pit that kneeling on the burning black rubber was excruciating. When we broke for lunch, everyone wearing shorts was given sanitary napkins to tie around their knees. By day's end we'd done only two more rolls of rubber. The next day we ran out of workers and rubber.

Fortunately the Carlisle Rubber Company was located just the other side of Hartford. Delighted to be relieved from the blistering heat of the pit, I offered to drive in for more rolls while Hank tried to figure out how to keep the rubber in place at the bottom of the retaining wall and up the wall itself. From then on Hank and I slaved alone in the pit, except when our kids came home on weekends to help.

The fact that not a single drop of rain fell during this whole project was a miracle. We'd had no idea it would take so long, but because the strips of rubber needed to be pie-shaped to fit the contours of the pond, it took forever to finish the last quarter of the pond. We used nine and a half rolls of rubber and glued together about 800 feet of seams.

Then to insure there'd never be a leak, we cut square patches to glue down over any place where two seams met - about fifty in all. Painting a two-foot square and its counterpart with glue wasn't bad, but by then October's first frost had occurred and the big maple next to the pond would inevitably let loose a dozen golden leaves to land on each freshly-painted patch, requiring us to pick off each separate leaf. My knees hurt just recalling all this agony.

On October 18th we started letting in the water, which had been diverted into a trench during the pond's construction. Our water supply was still limited, so it took more than a month to fill the pond to the brim, but in the ten years since then the water level has never gone down more than an inch, even during the most severe drought.

Despite the fact that it is lined with rubber, we refuse to treat the pond as a swimming pool. Spring rains and autumn winds have filled its bottom with silt and fallen leaves, and the apple tree plops its fruit into the water each fall. Even a great blue heron assumed it was a normal pond one summer day when he alighted on the bank, probably hoping to catch Susan, our enormous goldfish, named for her one black eye.

Such a foolish-looking bird with his stilt-like legs and long S-curved neck! He began to stalk very cautiously around the grassy bank, raising each long leg with infinite care and setting it down without a sound. After many minutes of diligent investigation, he chose a spot to enter the water, but his study of the terrain had missed one important fact – the pond was lined with rubber.

The heron's slow-motion movements abruptly changed to fast-forward as his front foot came in contact with slippery rubber. Have you ever seen a bird make a prat-fall? Those stilt-like legs went right out from under Mr. Heron as he flapped his great blue wings, frantically trying to catch his balance. You could almost see the embarrassment on his long silly face as he fumbled back to shore.

But he wouldn't give up. Time and time again he'd start into the water, then – Oops! Down he'd go in another prat-fall as his claws hit the slick slanting rubber. Finally he decided there was no easy meal to be had, flapped himself into the air and flew away.

Most of us fortunate enough to live in the country are well aware of the fringe benefits offered by our rural lifestyle. Crisp tender vegetables from the garden, fresh eggs with firm, orange yolks, sheets that smell of sunshine. The lush fields and restful blue mountains may be our everyday view, but we know they're pretty special.

We realize how lucky we are that we can get ready for bed without bothering to pull the shade and then be lulled to sleep by peepers and tree toads instead of police sirens and trucks gnashing their gears. We still thrill at the sight of deer grazing at dusk or wild geese dotting the sky at dawn.

What we tend to take for granted is all the knowledge we've acquired through this bucolic life, the ins and outs of country living we've absorbed over the years, and yes, let's face it, the drawbacks we've learned to put up with. City folk don't get bitten by a million black flies every May or run out of water in a dry August or lose their electricity with every other snowstorm.

The Taylor kids were brought up knowing all the little hazards of farm life, learning to shut gates and not drive across uncut hayfields, to separate paper trash from the cans and foil and plastic that must to be taken to the dump; that garbage goes on the compost pile; that leaving unpasteurized milk on the counter on a hot day is a no-no.

The reason I'm bringing all this up is that last weekend Hank and I were invited to the shore, and we reluctantly agreed to let daughter Bridget, who's been living in NYC for the past two years, bring a few friends home to Locust Hill while we were gone. It was a disaster! Not that the five city slickers didn't enjoy themselves – they had a grand time. It was only Bridget (and on our return, Hank and I) who considered the weekend a catastrophe.

The houseguests were thrilled with the view, fascinated by the vegetable garden and the animals, awed by the freezer full of homegrown meat, and completely ignorant of what keeps a farm running smoothly. They flung open a dozen windows without screens so that the house buzzed with flies and the areas around lights (obviously left on all night for some reason) turned into huge insect graveyards. Their feet made picturesque blotches of manure on most of the downstairs carpets. Rummaging in the chest freezer for steaks, they dislodged a freezer basket and consequently left the top open several inches, resulting in a dripping interior, not discovered until the following Tuesday.

The sheep, having found that the guests had left the gate unlatched, invaded the garden, trampling down the staked tomatoes and the bean rows, nibbling the tops off all the carrots, most of the beets and even a few onions, then completely demolishing three generations of lettuce plants.

The young ewe staked on the dam to play lawn mower was so spooked by the five city slickers trying to pet her that she broke her tether in a desperate attempt to get away from them. Too distraught to be caught, she was left to drag 6 feet of chain up and down the perennial border in front of the fence all day, trying to get into the pasture with the rest of the flock.

On Sunday, while Bridget frantically tried to remove rug stains and sort out the mess of paper plates and napkins from the beer bottles, corn cobs and other items dumped helter-skelter into the various wastebaskets, her guests took a nice long walk. Unfamiliar with our "Texas gates," they closed them all improperly and shortly afterward the three steers happily moved on to greener pastures.

By the time we got home, Bridget and her friends had returned to the big city – a good thing, as getting the steers home was a nightmare that used up all our patience. Stuffed from dining on our neighbor's corn in a lot three miles away, they wouldn't deign to even sniff at our bucket of grain. It wasn't until Wednesday that we got them home.

ROLL OUT THE GREEN CARPET

If you've ever seeded a lawn, watered it, fertilized it and tried to protect its tender beginnings from dogs, children and weed seeds, you know what a difficult task it is. The usual rewards found in "do-it-yourself" projects just aren't part of this job, especially if the end result is thin and dappled with dandelions. Hank and I had seeded many a lawn over the years, but when we finished the great rubber pond, it was too late in the year to plant grass seed.

Being serious "Do-it-Yourselfers," we might never have discovered the beauty of ready-made turf if we hadn't been faced with the raw dirt on the sloping banks of the new pond as September slipped into October. We could picture the banks eroding, washing soil into the pond all winter. With a turf farm not ten miles away, we decided to check out the cost of sodding the banks with the commercial variety.

To my delight I found that by getting "seconds" – the rolls that weren't exactly six feet long – the cost would be a better investment than wall-to-wall carpeting, at a fraction of the price. Where can you buy a rug for $1.59 a yard? Especially one impervious to red wine and cigarette burns!

Actually, we ended up getting all that green carpet for free as a thank-you for the complimentary article on turf that I wrote for Horticulture Magazine.

We Americans are so accustomed to fast-food hamburgers, overnight packages, and cars that zoom from 0 to 60 mph in ten second, that we've become impatient with waiting. If such luxuries as instant winter suntans are now available, why not instant lawns. I'm not partial to instant coffee or store-bought pies, much less TV dinners or sun-lamp tans, but ready-made grass has none of the drawbacks found in most instant products.

Laying out the green carpet is as easy as undoing a bedroll. No special preparation is necessary other than to provide a smooth, rock-free soil surface. We set each roll of sod (about thirty pounds) so it faced the right way and fit snugly against the last, then uncoiled it, making sure the seams fell in different places in each line.

When I tried lifting a section a week later, I found that dozens of white roots had already started to reach down and dig into their new home. The only problem was that all those pristine rolls of Kentucky blue grass made our other lawns look like something the cat dragged in.

And no wonder - the care given grass at a sod farm would be difficult for the average homeowner to duplicate. The grass is fertilized at least once a month during the growing season. Each spring, just before the lilacs bloom, Tupersan or Dacthal, pre-emergent crabgrass killers which will be effective all summer, are applied.

Naturally we offered our grass none of these helpful items. As a consequence it only took a few years for that beautiful weed-free lawn surrounding the pond to turn into something resembling the other lawns on Low Cost Hill. Jill-over-the-ground, plantains, dandelions – all the weeds in the neighborhood came over to play with the new kids from Kentucky.

I suspect, however, we'll never be able to bring ourselves to make another lawn the old-fashioned way, having experienced the joys of using commercially grown grass.

The American Agriculturist, first published in 1847, was edited for many years by a teetotaling gentleman named Orange Judd. In one of the early issues he wrote an article on cider that paints an amusing picture of New England.

"Cider making in the olden time was reckoned one of the important parts of farm labor…" the article begins. "The cider pitcher stood regularly upon the table at meal times, and the jug was a constant field companion. Happily that day is past. Experience has proved that more and better work can be done without than with alcoholic stimulants. Every exaltation of the feelings is followed by a corresponding depression, so that in the end there is no gain of strength from stimulants."

Making sweet cider (we never deliberately turned it into hard cider) was an annual event on Locust Hill when our children were still around. I shouldn't admit it, but I never enjoyed it much. Oh, I loved collecting the apples. I was as happy as a monkey climbing the old apple trees in our various neighbors' abandoned orchards and shaking down the fruit. We would spend most of a morning getting as many kinds of apples as we could, since blending different varieties to get just the right tartness or sweetness is what makes good cider.

Once home with our feed bags bursting from the trunk of the car, we'd haul out old Granddaddy Taylor's cider press from the long shed, wash off the guano from the summer's nesting barn swallows with the hose, and check to see which ancient part had warped, broken or disintegrated over the previous winter.

While Hank repaired or replaced the latest vital piece, the children and I would gather up the gallon jugs, the pot, the pitcher, the funnel and the cheesecloth, and hose off the apples. Then came the part I disliked. You may be thinking it was hand-cranking the apples through the masher, but Hank had motorized that process early on.

No, what I couldn't stand was helping to shove those wormy, splotched and scabby apples into the press. Bits of grass and leaves, greedy wasps, and other pieces of foreign matter went through the hungry spinning wheel with its jagged teeth, along with the apples. All were ground to a frothy pulp and spit out into the slatted container below.

The state health inspector would have turned green, not with envy, but with shock and loss of appetite at the ingredients that went into Taylor cider! I rarely participated in this part of the operation, busy with my layers of cheesecloth in the forlorn hope that straining would somehow eliminate the worms and other tidbits from the juice when it was funneled into the jugs.

The pressing process was not mechanized. We all took turns cranking down the giant screw, our sticky wet hands growing chill and numb in the crisp November air. The children watched the first sparkling juice flush through the slats, then eagerly passed the first glass of squeezings from one to another with smacking lips. I always hesitated, knowing what had gone into it, but each year I'd succumb in the end. It was inevitably delicious, sweet and clear, and twice as flavorful as the store-bought stuff.

By the time the sun slipped behind Canaan Mountain, we'd have ten or twelve jugs and a wheelbarrow full of punts. It was amazing how totally dry those punts were, every scrap of juice pressed out, leaving such a solid cake that Hank would have to bash it out of the container with a log. I would wheel the punts to the compost pile as dusk darkened the sky, Hank would hose down the press, and the kids would lug the jugs down to the cold cellar.

It was actually a lot of fun, now that I'm writing about it instead of doing it. And the result - gallons of fresh sweet cider and eventually fizzy aged cider - kept us in free refreshment all fall.

When I get so old I start driving my car at a cautious 30 mph, peering nervously at the oncoming traffic with half-blind eyes, I know I won't give up this last piece of independence any more gracefully than the current crop of doddery drivers. Hopefully before that day arrives, someone will design a proper car for the elderly.

I think it should be made out of some soft fungus material such as mushrooms, so that if we old folks are so senile as to hit something, we can't damage it – be it a tree, a telephone pole or a toddler. Obviously these mushroom cars would have no collision coverage, but their liability insurance would be very inexpensive. They could get us old geezers to the doctor or the hairdresser if we didn't want to ask someone to drive us or were too cheap to take a taxi.

Fungi might seem like weird materials to use in a vehicle, but they've been put to far stranger uses – it is a fungus that turns a lump of dough into an airy loaf of bread, another that makes whiskey from rye mash. Industrial products from fabrics to plastics include these non-plant, non-animal molds in their manufacture.

Of course the most popular fungi are the mushrooms. I don't eat wild mushrooms. The one time I came home and cooked some that I'd been given by my neighbor, a knowledgeable mushroom hunter, Hank took one look and quickly gave them to our chickens (who, I might add, ate them with relish and did not keel over dead).

What I do eat are puffballs. And so does Hank. They are one of the most delectable of the fungi. They are also one of the safest, as there are no poisonous varieties known. They are white in color, spherical in shape and their insides are uniformly firm and white. They are easily distinguished from other mushrooms as they have no stem, gills or cap.

The only possible danger with puffballs would be in mistaking a deadly Amanita in the "button" stage for a puffball, but this is easily checked by slicing the ball in half. If it's a puffball it will have no outline of stalk, gills or cap.

The giant puffball, *Calvatia maxima*, can be anywhere from the size of a softball to that of a basketball. If you've found one with its inside still pristinely white with no tinge of yellow, you've found an ambrosial treat. Take it home, slice it and sauté it in butter.

The puffball's edible period is so short that I'm forever coming across them too late, in the "puff" stage when the white ball has become a papery brown container. Kick it and the air fills with brown smoke, the microscopic spores that are the "seeds" of fungi. A level teaspoon of spores can contain 50 sextillion of them! When a single spore germinates it begins producing hyphae, the long filaments that form the mycelium. These fine threads grow so fast that a fungus can produce more than half a mile of them in a day! Eventually they produce fruiting bodies, be they puffballs, shaggy manes, morels or deadly amanitas.

Puffballs are terrestrial, living on the ground rather than on roots, bark or wood. They can be found in pastures or meadows, and appear from late July until October. Look for them a few days after a good soaking rain.

VEGETATION LITIGATION

Nowadays newspapers are full of litigation horror stories - a psychic suing her doctor for destroying her powers with a CAT scan, a mother blaming Little League for her son's clumsy catch. Being a mere housewife whose main occupation is gardening, I used to read such articles with interest but no apprehension, assuming I was safe from such irresponsible nonsense. I began to worry, however, when I learned that my neighbor had recently been sued by the weeping willow in her front yard.

This gnarled and arthritic old tree had reached the venerable age of ninety-two, despite a serious heart condition and the loss of several limbs. Last year my neighbor began giving the tree's roots large doses of fertilizer, and hired a tree surgeon to examine the damaged limbs. The willow sued her, charging that force-feeding would impede his right to die with dignity and that further amputations would only prolong his suffering.

The case resulted in an injunction that prohibited my neighbor from performing any and all heroic measures in the willow's behalf. When she asked the judge if she could just plumb chop the dying tree down and thus put him out of his misery, her request was denied.

Serious newspapers such as *The New York Times* or the *Wall Street Journal* rarely give space to such stories, but shortly after I heard about the willow case, a friend told me about a class-action suit recently filed somewhere in Vermont by a bed of perennials. Their grievance - the slum conditions under which they were forced to live. The chief instigators of the suit were the iris and phlox, but their lawyer had convinced them they'd have a much stronger case if other perennials in the bed became participants. The overcrowded astilbe and monarda, and even the delphiniums have agreed, but the peonies have chosen to appear as witnesses for the distraught gardener.

Another class-action suit that will have a substantial impact on homeowners is that of WEEDS VS. EPA in which a large group of noxious plants accused the Environmental Protection Agency of allowing the use of hazardous chemicals on lawns. The jury, including a majority of suburbanites, rendered a verdict of "not guilty". Unfortunately the judge, a strong advocate of wild life, reversed the decision, ruling in favor of the plaintiffs. The case is now being reviewed by the Supreme Court.

Just think of the snowball affect this sort of litigation can have. Soon sick plants will be demanding access to the best soils, gene-spliced seeds will sue scientists for destroying their self-worth, newly-planted saplings will be crying "whip-lash." Before we know it some fading flower will force the courts to decide on the constitutionality of "dead-heading!"

And you know what will happen to liability insurance - premiums will shoot up higher than Jack's beanstalk. Towns will stop improving their public parks with flower beds, and nurseries will give up raising difficult plants. We home gardeners might just have to throw in the trowel.

The thought of such devastating results prompted me to investigate further, and by pure luck I located an attorney who specializes in horticultural litigation. Mr. Green was quick to admit that there has been a wheelbarrow full of suits filed this past year, not only by flowers but also by vegetables. Rows of southern produce - collards, kale, okra and even sweet potatoes - have been suing New England gardeners for discrimination and unfair hiring practices.

Before we know it Yankee vegetables such as parsnips, turnips and lima beans will get into the act. Are all gardeners going to be forced to be equal-opportunity employers in the vegetable plot? Will we have to give good garden space to the useless male blossoms on our squash vines? Retain tired old beans until age 65?

In that case insurance companies will surely begin to exclude this type of liability coverage from their Homeowner policies, forcing backyard gardeners to "go bare." I'm afraid that would do little to stem the tide of litigation though. Attorneys handling such lawsuits would quickly find a "deep pocket" such as Burpee or Park to be respondent.

According to Mr. Green, the largest award won through vegetation litigation went to a crowd of daffodils. The bulbs had been planted upside-down on the Rockefeller estate by a newly hired gardener. Claiming pain and suffering from irreparable damage to their insides, the bulbs were advised by council to sue the Rockefellers rather than the gardener, on the "deep pocket" theory. They won over a million pounds of fertilizer. I didn't ask Mr. Green, who appeared to be bereft of a funny bone, whether his fellow advocate's contingency fee had been paid in kind.

These cases are very disturbing, but the news is not all bad. The trial in which a clematis vine sued UPS for damage in shipment ended in a hung jury. And when Horticulture Magazine was charged with libel by the Dandelion family, the jury deliberated for less than fifteen minutes to decide in favor of the periodical.

Recently an even more encouraging development occurred in New York, a state that has enacted specific tort laws to provide "good faith" immunity. The elderly defendant, Mrs. Potter, a dedicated gardener living on a fixed pension, was accused by her backyard vegetables of neglect and mismanagement.

Mrs. Potter's lawyer defended his client brilliantly, arguing that her age and physical stamina precluded the extreme nurturing called for by the plaintiffs; that the basic criteria of good gardening includes only planting, weeding, watering and harvesting, all of which had been performed; that the buying of fertilizer or hiring of a yard boy were beyond Mrs. Potter's means. His strongest protest, however, was that there had been absolutely no reckless or deliberate disregard of the care and safety of the vegetables.

Witnesses for the prosecution included several mud-splattered, unstaked tomato vines, two cauliflowers with severe sunburn, and a dozen undernourished beets. A scabby potato testified that his disfigurement had been caused by sour soil. (This testimony was contradicted the next day by a soil expert whose litmus tests of Mrs. Potter's dirt had a pH reading of 7.2.) The most damaging evidence was produced by a weeping head of lettuce who described in lurid detail the slime of slugs that had slithered into her row.

Despite this bushel of hostile witnesses, the jury remained sympathetic to the diminutive defendant. The fact that she stood under five feet in her sneakers, weighed little more than an overgrown zucchini and had eyes as blue as two delphiniums possibly helped them reach their decision, but their verdict of acquittal was completely justified.

POTTER VS. TOMATOES ET AL was a landmark decision. Provided more states take up "good faith" immunity, it will be the most promising defense for home gardeners. Since one of my peony plants was crushed by the post-hole digger this spring when we replaced a post backing the perennial border, I am hoping Connecticut enacts a similar tort law before I find myself in the dock.

GARDEN ORNAMENTS

Bartlett's Quotations doesn't reveal who first said "There's no accounting for tastes," but as far as I'm concerned one's upbringing can, in large part, be held accountable. If we're talking about taste buds, for instance, I was raised on custard cooked too quickly so that it curdled (my mom was a great gardener, but not a very good cook) and got addicted to the nubbly texture. I can't stand smooth, creamy custard. I'm sure if I'd been a Southerner raised on grits and okra, I'd find them delicious.

Defining taste as it concerns more esoteric items such as works of art, literature or clothing styles, is a more nebulous task. No two human beings have totally similar ideas of what constitutes good or bad taste. That's what makes life so interesting. If everyone felt like I did, there'd be no plastic flowers or open-toed shoes or blue Christmas lights.

When I was a child I adored the kind of garden statues that decorated a few of the front lawns in West Hartford – baby ducks in a row, plastic pink flamingos drinking at a birdbath, colorful elves in a flower bed. I could never understand why my mother didn't care to have such ornaments dotting the front yard – or even the back yard.

I can't remember when I came to the conclusion that I didn't want them either, but I'm sorry. I've deprived myself of the fun and excitement I used to feel at the sight of a plastic deer in someone's garden, or an elf sitting on a giant polka-dotted toadstool.

To each his own, or to mix up a couple of quotations, " 'One man's poison is another man's meat and drink' said the old lady as she kissed the cow." I'm glad there are folks out there who want plastic pink flamingoes in their yard, or that polka-dotted lady bending over in the flower bed. Some of the garden ornaments carried in the catalogs nowadays are truly amazing, but they're not things I want on Locust Hill.

Did that change turn me into a snob? I just looked up the word "snob" in the dictionary and was surprised to find that the first meaning of the word is "a cobbler or shoemaker." But even the other meanings were not what I'd thought. "Not of the aristocracy; a commoner, one who imitates the upper classes." Fascinating!

Well, I'd rather be a commoner than an aristocrat any day, so I won't worry the point. What brought up this statue bit was several things. The first was deciding that my Alotta garden, which I've never been too happy with, might look better if I put some sort of statue at the back that would give a point to the pool and lure the visitor's eye to that corner of the garden.

But what sort of statue? Having been influenced by people whose opinions I respect, I no longer wanted cutsie little people in the garden. I decided that a garden statue should be well proportioned, unpainted, and if not original, a good copy of an original. A few weeks later I saw a classified ad that read "Cement lawn statues – large, hand-painted, drunken Charlie, cigarstore Indian, small donkeys, Jesus, etc." I saved the ad because even though it didn't sound quite like what I was looking for, it was a perfect illustration of what's available in the way of statuary.

It was daughter Trum, poking around at tag sales, who found the figure that now stands in the far corner of the Alotta garden between the two back walls. He's entitled "Winter" and is a nicely weathered gray, having obviously faced snow and ice for many years.

Somewhere I feel sure he has a sister called "Summer," but until I find her I'm happy to have Winter in my garden all year round.

All good gardeners know that it's not just a mistake, but an unpardonable sin to go through the fall without planting something new, something to delight and surprise the eye come spring - bulbs, a flowering shrub, a fruit tree. It's not too late. If it's too cold today, tomorrow may produce Indian summer, and not getting outside during Indian summer is another unpardonable sin.

In my ancient copy of <u>Facts for Farmers</u>, missing its cover and so tattered and torn I can't find its publication date, there's a wonderful description of crocuses in the chapter titled " Bulbous Flowering Plants."

"Crocuses enamel the lawn or make the garden lovely with their stainless purity. ... these firstlings of the season have a special claim to the popular regard, the harbingers of buds and blossoms, leafy trees and unbound waters...These little pilgrims silently yet eloquently, assure us that we are entering upon a new cycle of bland airs and fragrant odors. We believe in their humanizing influences. They are entitled to receive the most cordial welcome."

What flowery old-fashioned folderol, but there's no doubt that crocuses are appealing. So are all the other bulbous plants. Once planted, they will continue to bloom for years and produce plenty of offspring. Of course there's always an exception to the rule – in this case it's tulips. These bulbs rarely last more than a year or two. Unlike daffodils or narcissus or jonquils that are poisonous, tulips are gobbled up each winter by field mice.

Gardeners often think moles are the culprits when they see tunnels bumping along under the soil and no tulips grace the garden the following spring, but moles are carnivores. They're only interested in bugs. It's the vegetarian field mice who dine on tulip bulbs. They use the mole tunnels to get underground.

I've never had much luck with tulips, but when Bridget, our middle daughter, got engaged and set her wedding date for mid-May, she and I planted several dozen tulips in front of the area where the tent would be, along with daffodils and other spring bloomers. They looked very colorful on the wedding day, but that fall, not wanting to care for yet another flower bed, I planted the area with pachysandra.

Both the tulips and the daffodils continue to come up and bloom each spring. I wasn't surprised about the daffodils, but I was delighted with the tulips. Neither mice nor moles seem to care to struggle through all those pachysandra roots. Other ways to protect your bulbs from becoming dinner for the mice include planting them in pots or wrapping them in pot scrubbers or surrounding them with mothballs.

Several years ago some friends of ours were given a "Bulb Bash," a housewarming present that would warm any gardener's heart. They'd just moved into their newly built house, and that weekend a dozen friends arrived carrying bushels of bulbs along with a gas-powered posthole digger.

Using a mechanical digger to plant flower bulbs might seem a bit extreme, like using a sledge hammer to put in a thumbtack, but we're talking a total of 1200 bulbs! Each friend who'd contributed to this house present had brought 100 bulbs – daffodils, narcissus, crocuses, snowdrops, scillas, even some bright red tulips.

The next spring the yard was alive with flowers. Doesn't this "Bulb Bash" make a fabulous house present?

We've just enjoyed a rare day when all the kids were home at once. How times change. When I was a kid, our family, along with all our uncles and aunts and cousins, went to lunch every Sunday at Grandmother Cookie's house. When it rained we built complicated mansions out of playing cards and poker chips under the dining room table, or snuck up to Cookie's mirrored dressingroom to exchange our velvet dresses and patent leather shoes for satin nightgowns and chiffon scarves and wobbly, pointy-toed high heels.

These rainy day games were fun, but my fondest memories are of the sunny Sundays when we played outside. The game I remember best was called "Garden." You probably think I made that up just to get around to my proper subject, but it really was called "Garden" and furthermore, I think it was responsible for my first awakenings to the beauties of nature.

"Garden" was played on the stone wall surrounding Cookie's house. This was not your average stone wall. It was topped with cut flagstones about three inches thick and three feet square, and marched around the entire yard. In most places it was table height, but as it turned the corner toward the kitchen it grew step-by-step until it was high enough to hide the clothesline and trash bins, bowed out to avoid a giant sycamore, then stepped back down to normal height.

Every time I think of that wall, I wonder what happened to all those incredible cut stones when the city of Hartford tore down my grandmother's house and replaced it with a huge high school.

When my favorite cousin and I played "Garden," we'd begin by each picking one of those beautiful flat stones to be our own special table garden. A choice stone might be one overhung with azalea blossoms or shiny rhododendron leaves. Even better, one decorated with moss or slightly scalloped so it could hold water and resemble a tiny lake. Once this momentous decision was made, we'd go off to find the treasures to fill our garden.

Now you must remember, we were only seven or eight, and just discovering the strange and exotic mysteries that adults take for granted. Finding a red toadstool covered with spots was very exciting. So was the discovery of a tiny emerald fern or a giant palm-shaped leaf, close to fifteen inches across, from a horse chestnut tree. And I can still remember the thrill I felt the first time I pried open a thick prickly husk from under the horse chestnut tree and found the smooth mahogany nut inside, marbled with white.

The treasures we chose to put in our gardens required an adventurous search over acres of landscaped grounds - through the rose garden, among the exotic shrubs and trees surrounding the lawns, down the crooked stone steps by the potting shed where Willie, the gardener, hung out, to the vegetable garden and the herb garden, as well as the meadow, the wood and the river (forbidden territory).

A September garden might include such jewels as an orange fungus clinging to a twig, a bluejay feather, a strange gall malforming the stem of a goldenrod, a glossy beetle kept in the garden by a wall of pebbles or pinecones, a cluster of red dogwood berries; a single long skinny catalpa bean (very hard to acquire since the branches of that particular tree were hard to reach,) or a velvety seed pod from Cookie's wisteria vine.

Once the treasures were collected, we arranged them artistically (very important) on the flagstone we'd chosen and invited each other to view and admire them, then barter certain prize items for others not in our own collection. This may sound like a silly game, but viewed through the eyes of a child, it was very special. And I haven't a doubt that it was what first opened my eyes to the excitement to be found in Nature's garden.

What incredible improvements have been made by plant breeders since the first brave caveman – possibly the adjective hungry would be better – nibbled on the bitter, branching root of a wild carrot, or had the imagination to try eating a young thistle, the ancestor of our artichoke.

Today's vegetables have been derived from every single organ in the plant world, from roots and rhizomes to stalks, leaves, buds, blossoms and fruits. Now you and I might have been bright enough to try eating leaves like lettuce and spinach, or fruits such as squash and beans, but would we have thought to chomp down on a stem, the part of a plant we eat in celery, leeks and asparagus?

We all know what part of a potato vine is edible, but I bet quite a few folks died from eating the poisonous potato fruits, which look like a cluster of green cherries, before anyone thought to try consuming the knobby tubers hidden beneath the soil. We can thank some innovative primitive for trying to peel an onion, open up a melon or taste the immature flower of a broccoli plant.

The ancestors of today's vegetables contained toxic substances needed to protect them from insects and foraging animals. It wasn't until plants were raised in cultivation that these toxins were no longer needed for survival and man could begin to eliminate them.

Actually it was undoubtedly man's better half who bothered to plant the first seeds in her back yard. She may have done it by mistake, dumping seeds along with the dinner leftovers, but when they sprouted, she had the smarts to nurture them. She weeded and watered them, maybe even fertilized them. All these efforts improved their quality, but even more important, it allowed her to save the seeds from the very best plants to be sown the next year.

The great debate over whether heredity or environment is more influential in forming a human being's character may never be solved, and the same can be said about plant life. I always thought environment was more influential until the gene-splicers started manipulating flowers and vegetables faster than you can eat a fuzzless peach or peel a tearless onion. Still, environment plays a large part in the changes occurring in nature.

Darwin's theory - the survival of the fittest - couldn't work without the effects of environment as well as heredity. The moth that avoids being spotted by a bird because her wings are camouflaged to look like the bark of a tree lives to pass along that gene to the next generation in the eggs she lays. The flower that adapts itself to pollination by a different species of bee when its regular pollinator has died out, passes that trait on in its seeds.

One of the best examples of the changes created in the plant kingdom by both heredity and environment is found in *Brassica oleracea*. It may seem hard to believe, but this single species has evolved into nine variations - broccoli, Brussels sprouts, kale, collards, cauliflower, kohlrabi, and three different cabbages - savoy, red and green. The cabbage family is not a family, not even a genus, but a species that has produced nine subspecies.

Most of these varieties of *B. oleracea* start life with a pair of heart-shaped leaves. All the seedlings are so similar that we amateur gardeners have trouble telling them apart. As they mature, however, their leaves, stems or roots produce distinctive differences. Some shorten the petioles of their leaves so that each grows closer together than the last, creating the vegetable we call cabbage. Other varieties form a loose crown of leaves producing either kale or collards.

Another variety swells its stem into a crunchy edible bulb known as kohlrabi, while another has been influenced to produce tight tender flower buds we label broccoli, or the bleached sub-variety cauliflower. The last variation, Brussels sprouts, swells its axillary buds into tiny cabbages.

All nine subspecies of *B. oleracea* contain bitter chemicals called glucosinolates. Savoy cabbage has a great many of these chemicals, giving it a strong flavor, while red cabbage has very few, allowing it to have a bland taste. All nine also contain heaps of vitamin C and are low in calories, provided you don't lather them in butter or mayonnaise.

Although all the Brassicas like a soil rich in nitrogen, phosphorus and potassium, these nutrients must be provided from day one for cauliflower, broccoli and the cabbages because the outer leaves store them for future use from the very beginning. When these plants begin their last stage of growth, they do it so rapidly that the roots can't keep up with the supply, so it is the outer leaves that make the short transfer of minerals during this last stage.

Cabbages have one serious enemy, the flea beetle, who moves into the garden early in the season and adores tender tiny seedlings. Rather than starting seeds in the garden, plant six-week old seedlings that can withstand a little nibbling by the flea beetle. Planting a few turnips nearby is another control, as flea beetles prefer their leaves over those of cabbage. I've never raised any of the cabbages. What can you do with an entire row of cabbages anyway? Make sauerkraut, I suppose.

THE INSTANT GARDEN

The object of starting seeds indoors is to give them a head start and a longer growing season than they would get outside. Vegetables like tomatoes and melons need this early start, but vegetables that grow rapidly or tolerate cold weather or are difficult to transplant, should all be planted directly in the garden.

All this may seem obvious, but may not be to a beginning gardener. Trum, the only one of our three daughters who has become a serious gardener, started a vegetable garden as soon as she was married. That first year she asked me all about raising seedlings - what kind of potting soil to use, how much light and water, how to "harden off" - but she never asked, and I never thought to tell her, which seeds to plant.

Trum started every vegetable she planned to have in her garden indoors - not only tomatoes and broccoli and onions, but peas, beans, spinach, corn, pumpkins and carrots! When I saw all these flats I was chagrined, but the last thing I wanted was to dampen a budding gardener's enthusiasm, so we planted all the seedlings in what was quickly dubbed The Instant Garden.

Can you picture it? We started in the morning with a plot of empty soil and at the end of the day we had eight full rows of growing greenery. Knowledgeable gardeners just don't get that kind of instant success, and the fact is they don't want it.

Trum's bean plants had grown so fast indoors that they were eight inches high, but as sick and spindly as calves with the scours. They filled a long row of the Instant Garden, but they were so shook up by the move that they sat numbly in their new home for two whole weeks before they felt secure enough to start growing again. Had we been ruthless enough to throw them away and plant fresh seeds directly in the garden, the new plants would have been just as high in a few weeks and in far better shape to produce beans.

Trum's two flats of baby carrots made a pretty row of lacy greenery, but when she harvested them, they were so crooked they could have been worn as bracelets. The peas and spinach went into shock after being transplanted, reviving just in time to be wilted by hot weather. The corn stood up well under the move, as did the tomatoes, broccoli and onions, but the pumpkin vines just curled up and died. Pumpkins should always be planted in their permanent home.

Trum's first garden was not exactly a roaring success in the end, but that didn't spoil the fact that it was definitely one in the beginning. We had a great many giggles as we planted The Instant Garden. Having a daughter as enthusiastic about gardening as her Mom has been a delight.

Trum now lives in Oregon where the weather is so temperate she can plant tender crops outdoors in February. She can leave her dahlias and gladiolus in the ground all winter. I'm always green with envy when I talk to her in March when New England is either in the midst of a blizzard or sitting in mud and Oregon is bursting with daffodils and tulips, and Trum has just come in from picking her asparagus.

On the other hand, when I talk to her in June and find it's been raining steadily for two weeks in Oregon, I thank my lucky stars I live where I do. We may have a short growing season, but it's usually a sunny one.

THE ARTIST'S GARDEN

In 1987 I discovered our freezer still contained six packages of vegetables I'd put up in 1984. Having a large garden is a boon when you're trying to feed a family of five, but the Taylor eating habits had been changing radically as we married off one daughter after another. It was time to shrink the garden to fit our shrinking appetites.

What better place to begin a flower garden than an area that had been tilled and manured, weeded and watered for five years? I decided I wanted a dizzying display of country flowers that would be totally different from my rather formal perennial border. I bought something called "The Artist's Garden," a collection of 150 varieties of flowers Claude Monet had planted at Giverny, his famous garden outside Paris. The seed containers were laid out on a palette as if they were paint samples – annual/blue/short, perennial/yellow/tall, annual/red/pink/medium, etc.

There were no directions on how to plant all those specks, spirals and spots of unidentified life. Scattering hundreds of seeds around the garden as if I were feeding my chickens their nightly ration of corn was a frightening idea, but the alternative - raising 500 seedlings in flats – sounded even worse..

The design instructions read "Do what you think will look good. There are no rules." Hmm. I've never been fond of rules, but in this case I could have used some.

When the soil finally warmed up in late May, I broadcast each container of seeds over the loosened soil, scattering the tall varieties toward the garden's edges, the short ones close to the paths and the in-betweeners in between. So much for design. Then I gently raked the area and sprinkled four or five buckets worth of compost over the seeds.

By then it was raining. Perfect! Now all I had to do was wait. At the end of a week, tiny green plants began to pop up. The first ones were easy to recognize - sour grass, quack grass, bedstraw, clover, pigweed, - all the weeds I'd been pulling in the vegetable garden for years. But then minuscule pieces of unidentifiable greenery appeared. The Monet seeds had begun to sprout.

I decided not to pull up any seedling I couldn't identify. Each night I studied the names on the Monet list and poured over my garden books, trying to find pictures of the plants I was unfamiliar with or whose Latin names meant nothing to me. The pictures I located were no help at all, since each was of a mature blossoming plant, not a seedling.

As the weeks went by, the job of weeding became both physically and mentally exhausting. Was this a baby baby's breath or a young bedstraw? Was that a good member of the pea family or a bad one? I felt like Sherlock Holmes, magnifying glass in hand. The only areas of the garden I could weed without an identity crisis were the paths.

That first year, two of the most prominent flowers in the garden had actually come from my own flower border via the compost I'd spread - feverfew, a miniature white and yellow chrysanthemum that blooms throughout the summer, and an annual pink poppy. By July the garden

142

was a dazzling display of poppies poking their pink faces through the crowds of little white chrysanthemums. It wasn't Monet's garden. It was mine. Only one flower from the Monet collection, Anchusa, an annual sky-blue forget-me-not, joined my own contributions that month.

By August, however, other plants finally got into the act - yellow coreopsis falling all over itself, Clary sage with white bracts veined in threads of purple, delicate blue Campanulas, flashes of red from the tassels of Love-lies bleeding, Amaranthus. By September there were few spaces left for unwanted weeds. The crowded jumble of color I'd pictured for my country garden had become a reality.

The perennials in the Monet collection began contributing their flowers to the garden the following summer. Despite being scattered like chicken feed, an amazing number of them not only germinated, but managed to survive the crowded conditions - lupines, yarrows, Shasta daises, rudbeckias, plus many more with less familiar names.

The first to bloom were the granny bonnet columbines, their rich maroon and white flowers reaching up on delicate stems above their blue-green foliage. They were followed by a magnificent show of tall, phlox-like flowers in lavender and white. With fifteen flowers listed under tall, white/blue/lavender perennials, it took me half the summer to be sure these handsome plants were *Campanula latifolia.*

Next the sweet Williams, which had been only nondescript bunches of leaves for almost a year, were sporting blossoms in every shade of pink to red; creamy spires of foxgloves were up and luring the bees; clouds of baby's breath were filling up with tiny white stars.

As each month came and went, more and more flowers showed themselves. Walking around the garden almost always brought another discovery. Solving the mysteries of the unknown perennials that had haunted me most of the previous summer was as delightful as learning as a young mother whether you've produced a boy or a girl.

143

One plant in particular had frustrated me ever since it first twined its long delicate stems around a clump of silver-gray lamb's ears. It looked like nothing more than a weed, but like all the other unknowns, I'd resisted pulling it. Since almost every clump of lamb's ears contained a similar little vine, I hoped it would prove to be something special.

The next April it looked as weedy as ever, but by late May I was rewarded for my patience. Tiny pink blossoms opened their eyes as they nestled in their bed of soft gray leaves - *Gypsophilia repens-rosea*, a creeping baby's breath.

I had less success with another thready vine I eventually nicknamed "Monet's Revenge," since it looked unlike any weed I knew. I left it and all its brothers and sisters alone. By September, well hidden by taller, more substantial plants, these vines had secretly bloomed (minute white flowers even less interesting than those of chickweed) and gone to seed, so that by the next June hundreds of their offspring were tangling around the feet of neighboring plants. Getting rid of these no-name weeds was harder than unsnarling kite string from a privet hedge.

The job of weeding was very different once the garden was well established. I spent much of my time getting rid of ordinary field flowers that had been included in the Monet collection - hawkweed, bouncing Bet, potentilla, morning glory (a glorified name for bindweed)- none of which I felt deserved space in the garden. I suppose if you lived in France where such common flowers aren't common, you would treasure them, but I didn't think they stood up well against showier flowers like foxgloves and lupines.

The third summer I wrote an article for Fine Gardening Magazine about the garden, and weeded, watered and dead-headed diligently so the flowers would look their best when the photographer came to take their picture. One picture turned out to be good enough to be used as the cover of the magazine, and the publisher was kind enough to let me use it for the cover of this book as well.

No garden can survive without constant care. Merely keeping it weeded and watered was not enough. By the fourth summer almost all the annuals in the collection had disappeared, as had the rarer perennials. I worked diligently, and a little desperately, to recreate the previous summers' glories, adding compost and annuals, but by the fifth summer the most ordinary plants - heliopsis, monarda, milfoil and violets - had completely overrun the garden, ousting the more delicate one-of-a-kind treasures that had made the garden so exciting. I decided it was time to eliminate this monument to work and weeding.

Daughter Bridget and her spouse (by far the brightest and nicest of those city slickers she'd brought out for the weekend) had just built a small cottage across the meadow as a weekend escape from Manhattan, so I was able to actually enjoy the dismantling of the garden. Bridget and I dug up a dozen different plants and transplanted them to the cottage. Bridget is the least garden-minded of the children, and consequently it was double fun to get her started down the perennial path.

I also invited every gardening friend I could think of to come and take away whatever they wanted or needed, and soon the backyard was pockmarked with potholes. After Hank had rototilled and we'd raked and seeded, the backyard once again became a boring lawn.

In the five years that I had the Monet garden, my feelings about it ran the gamut from furious frustration to ecstatic enthusiasm. Excitement, exhaustion, chagrin over my ignorance - I felt every imaginable emotion except boredom. I still miss the lush extravagance of picking daily bouquets to fill the house, the view of hummingbirds sipping nectar from the shaggy red bee balm, the excitement of discovering a new and different blossom. But it's nice having the time to play another set of tennis on a summer afternoon instead of slaving amongst the flowers of Monet.

Those dang weathermen! Relying on their forecasts is as chancy as trying to skinnydip at noon. An unpredicted shower washes out my tennis game as often as an unexpected deliveryman cuts short my mid-day swim. Too often when I listen to a weather report claiming a sunny day and rush to do the week's laundry, the sun vanishes behind a rain cloud just as I've pinned the last shirt on the line.

How can one decide to cut a hayfield or plan a picnic based on a 30% chance of thunderstorms? George Ford's heifers, who spend their summers in the Locust Hill pastures, are far more reliable at predicting showers than those TV fellas. If the herd of young Holsteins drifts down to the sheltering pines at the pasture's lower corner, their favorite spot for weathering rain squalls, it's a guarantee that before long the cloudless sky will be filled with ominous thunderheads.

Yesterday I was sitting under the maple tree about four, collecting myself after an afternoon of babysitting my two grandsons. I looked across the big meadow and saw those black and white cows gamboling along behind the pasture fence like so many thrown dice and I knew it was time to gather the books and toys and towels before they got wet.

Sure enough, within the next few minutes, the frogs began their counterpoint of croaks and chuggarums, the happy chorus that also precedes a thunderstorm. The pond's sunny sparkle vanished as its surface stilled, becoming dark and glassy, except where a pair of tree swallows dipped and soared above it, gathering a last-minute snack of insects before the storm.

The wind suddenly puffed at the lush green sumacs at the pasture's edge to display their silvery undersides, then hurried on across the meadow, rippling the green sea of timothy and broom and setting the rose pink clover blossoms dancing.

I watched as the blue shadows of Canaan Mountain misted into a shroud of gray gauze as the curtain of rain started up the valley, its growing murmur of sound barely heard against the leaves whispering together in excitement above my head. The first tentative splots of rain dotted the pond and rumbles of thunder echoed against the mountain. Single raindrops pinged against the sun-warmed flagstones of the terrace and evaporated, but soon dozens more drummed down in earnest. The storm had arrived.

The sky boiled with dark, wind-blown clouds. Jagged bolts of silver cut through the darkness in silent splendor, soon shattered by horrendous claps of thunder. Closer and closer, until a final spike of lightening smashed to earth too close for comfort. The air was heavy with the tangy odor of ozone. I forsook my chair under the maple and dashed through the downpour to the safety of the front porch, joining Bigger, the only dog we've ever had who enjoys thunderstorms.

That violent crack of thunder had obviously been the storm's finale. Off to the west, the darkness was already being chased away by blue sky. The rain was turning into a veil of pewter mist in the distance as it continued to drift toward Norfolk. The flagstones began to steam as the sun reappeared.

Ah, and there was the rainbow, curving its technicolor ribbon across the valley, a half-moon that must end in the pot of gold hidden behind the tower on Haystack Mountain. The day's oppressive heat had been swept away, and the whole world sparkled with greens of every shade.

The heifers were already starting their trek back along the fence toward the other end of the pasture. They'll not return to the pine grove until Mother Nature brews up another thunderstorm. Lightening has struck many a tree of Locust Hill, but never one of the heifers' pines. Do cows know something we don't?

Different gardens need different paths. Our raspberry bed's paths are made from old strips of carpeting. They're great at keeping down the weeds, but not exactly attractive. Paths made of bricks in intricate patterns are very attractive, but not for very long in New England where frost and weeds turn them into crumbled shards.

A well-mowed, well-edged grass path isn't very practical unless you have a well-paid gardener to mow and edge it. When I created The Artist's Garden in the back yard I was in a quandary as to what sort of paths to make for it. The paths Monet had at Giverny were made of small pebbles, but besides being expensive, how would I remove them if I decided to change their placement?

What my imagination would not stop visualizing was a quaint, curving path of stepping stones. With nothing but cobblestones on Locust Hill, I decided to make my own "stones" out of cement.

Hank and I have laid a lot of foundations, cinderblock walls and concrete floors over the years. Our cement mixer, one of the few big purchases we made in our first romantic year of married life, is crusted with gray splotches, its handle broken, its motor usually too tired to start turning the cone without a helping hand. But it still sloshes around cement, sand and water sufficiently to produce pretty nice concrete.

I found enough lumber scraps left over from other projects to cut 2" strips for frames. I built five identical forms, but instead of making them into 15"x24" rectangles, I canted one of the two short sides, making it 18" long. When laying the finished "stones" next to each other, the extra 3" produced a natural curve in the path.

I set my frames on a plastic sheet on the dirt floor of the shed, then cut chicken wire to fit each one for reinforcing. Heavier wire would have been better, but I was too cheap to buy any. Before mixing my cement, I placed an oak or maple leaf, a fern or, prettiest of all, a lupine leaf down on the plastic. They'd already been pressed flat in a heavy book. I put my first shovelful of cement down very gently so the plant material would remain flat and would pull off easily once the stone was turned right-side-up.

A good mason uses the same sort of technique as a good cook. I make a lot of casseroles as much by taste and smell as by measurement. I make cement as much by sound and sight. Cement that's the right consistency gives a certain thunk as it rounds the bend inside the cone, a certain plop as it is dumped. A too rich mix sounds sleek, one with too much sand sounds gritty, one too wet makes a gurgling slosh.

The hardest part is waiting for the cement to cure. Impatience doesn't pay. The cement must be kept damp for at least three or four days. I removed the frames from my first two "stones" too soon and cracked both of them. It took me two months to pour the 26 uncracked stones I needed for the Monet garden.

They wind their way through the flowers from the backdoor to the garden shed, and the imprints of leaves and ferns on their wavery surfaces look like fossils.

WHEN YOU SELL YOUR HOUSE

Back in 1988 when my 94-year-old mother went to the great garden in the sky, my sister and I put her house on the market. The question of whether it was legal or proper or stupid or unfair to take this shrub or that plant, this stone urn or that handsome flagstone bench popped up every single time I drove into West Hartford in my pickup truck. The fact is, anything goes, if it goes before you sell.

When I was growing up, our house sat on a 10-acre parcel of land, but over the years my family sold off most of that land so that only an acre remained. That acre was chuck full of things that I wanted to have on Locust Hill, from the expensive brass bird on the outdoor faucet to the great iron pot Mother kept planted with geraniums each summer. Happily, my sister had little interest in these items.

A portion of the yard was hidden from the house by a landscaped planting of rhododendrons and laurel. Left to its own devices, this area had turned into a jungle of escaped pachysandra and self-seeded pine trees. Remembering well the huge red-brown Connecticut Valley stones that formed a terrace in this portion of the yard when I was a child, I poked around in the thick carpet of pachysandra and found nine of them, the biggest measuring over 10 feet around.

Who would know they'd ever been there, if I could peel back the layers of pachysandra and remove them? It was a terrible temptation, and when my sister said "Go ahead!" I decided to do it. That night I called our bulldozer man, Elihu, and asked if he'd consider the project. Manipulating nine 5-inch thick flat rocks onto a trailer and carting them from West Hartford to East Canaan was just the sort of crazy idea that appealed to Elihu, if it could be done on a rainy day when he wasn't out on a bulldozing job.

Before the week was out we got our rainy day. I drove my little pickup and Elihu his big one with a flatbed trailer behind, plus chains, oak planks, two "Come-alongs"

(Elihu's term for a block and fall,) and a chainsaw. In 15 minutes the pine trees blocking our way to the rocks were down, cut up and stacked, and the work of hauling begun.

I'd assumed the job would be a mammoth one, like trying to get a refrigerator full of food up the stairs to a second floor apartment, but it was no more difficult than coaxing a reluctant puppy into a car. What a fantastic amount of leverage one can get with those little pulleys!

Once Elihu had snaked a chain around a stone, he'd work the handle of the Come-along like some frantic gambler playing a slot machine, while his son and I guided the rock inch by inch up the oak planks into the truck. It took barely two hours to load all nine stones, five in Elihu's truck, three in his trailer and one in my pickup.

Before the summer was out and just in time for our last daughter's wedding, Tam and her husband-to-be (no one is more eager to please than a future son-in-law) and I had manhandled all nine until they formed a beautiful curved staircase leading from the front lawn down to the terrace at the edge of the pond. (Hank was recovering from one of his many surgeries, this time a quadruple by-pass.) Tam in her high heels and bridal gown and Hank with his cane, both managed to totter down the stairs for the wedding ceremony.

Those huge flat stones solved a major landscape problem, but what I found particularly appealing is that 50 years ago those same stones had made another stairway, one that led from my grandparents' summer cottage down to the Farmington River. When the Barkhamsted Reservoir was built, flooding their cottage along with everything else in the valley, my parents decided those handsome red rocks should be saved and had them carted to West Hartford.

Now that I think about it, I guess I'm no more crazy than anyone else in our family. Lugging those great red rocks to East Canaan just kept a family tradition alive into the third generation.

I don't watch a lot of commercial television, mainly because I cannot stand the ads. Why do women get blamed for "ring around the collar" for instance, when the fact is that if men bothered to wash their necks once in a while, any old detergent would get their shirts clean?

And it's not just women who get it in the neck, the old folks do, too. Maybe it's because I just celebrated another aging birthday, but it seems to me that no one on TV over 30 drinks Pepsi or drives sporty new cars. You'd think the older generation had nothing to live for but head colds, sleepless nights, and getting seeds stuck in their dentures.

The day before my 50th birthday, my back went out of whack for the first time, and I must admit I suddenly felt some reservations about passing the half-century mark. Despite those continuing back problems, I find life on the other side of 50 more satisfying than ever.

Thanks to an incredible book <u>Drawing on the Right Side of the Brain</u> by Betty Edwards, I learned to draw at age 50. And in discovering how to turn on that intuitive relaxing right side of my head, I opened up a whole new world for myself. Among other things, I learned to enjoy swimming – definitely a right-brained activity. Swimming is my solution for a bad back, but you need to switch off the left brain and daydream if you want to do laps without going out of your mind with boredom.

Most folks I know find life on the other side of 50 pretty super, so why do TV ads denigrate the elderly? You'd think becoming a senior citizen was on a par with becoming a welfare mother. The brief moments of contentment I managed to snatch as a young mother stretch into whole weeks nowadays.

You know, I bet if those advertising executives took up gardening they'd change their attitude toward the elderly. Gardeners know enough to appreciate the values of age.

We don't think a young tree is imposing or august, in fact we consider it a characterless whip, naked, wimpy. It doesn't even provide much shade. But once it attains maturity, we give it adjectives like majestic and magnificent.

If the bark of an elderly oak gets lined and wrinkled, we think it handsome. We don't offer it skin creams like Night of Olay! When we see gnarled and twisted roots spreading out from the mighty trunk of a maple, we don't instantly think of Arthritic Pain Formula. When a paper birch is finally old enough for its bark to turn from brown to white, we don't insist it use Grecian Formula or Loving Care.

New garden soil is nothing to brag about, but after being fed good organic material summer after summer, it is rich in nutrients and minerals and is able to provide nourishment to the plants grown in it. The same can be said about the minds of older people. They've been acquiring knowledge and experience for years.

That's especially true of gardeners. Beginning gardeners know hardly anything, but as they continue working with Mother Nature they soak up more and more information about their plants. I was so ignorant about flowers when I was first married that when I was given a bouquet of peonies by a neighbor I had to ask what they were. Most gardeners are as familiar with this immortal perennial as gourmets are with garlic, but I'd never seen one before. Noting my enthusiasm, my neighbor offered to give me some roots.

"Come over on September 28th," she said as she was leaving. It being mid-June, I looked slightly puzzled. "That's the day I dig peonies," she explained. "My family had a crusty old gardener who said it was the only day they should be moved. He had a phenomenal green thumb. Everything he touched flourished, and I've always tried to follow his advice."

I've known quite a few young gardeners whose peonies never bloomed because they were planted either too deeply or too shallowly. I'm sure the peonies I transplanted to my garden would never have bloomed if I hadn't heeded the advice passed down to that neighbor by her crusty old gardener – how and where to dig the hole, how to set the "eyes" exactly 2 inches below the surface of the soil.

Actually, here in the northwest corner of Connecticut we need to plant our peonies about September 18th, so they have time to settle down before winter, but only age and experience taught me that.

Gardeners are close enough to nature to have a certain respect for age, be it a bonsai or a bougainvillea, a pine tree or a person. I can name dozens of things I prefer when they've aged, from crooked old houses and comfortable old shoes to ancient craggy rocks and vintage wine. I don't mind being called an old lady (far better than a senior citizen,) but I would also like to be pictured as having something more in my head than seeds in my teeth.

VOTE FOR THE GARDENER
OF YOUR CHOICE

I think Woody Woodpecker would have an easier time running for office in the political climate of today than anyone else. I'm awfully glad I deal in plants instead of politics! If my vegetables could vote, I'd probably be out of a job. They'd choose some gardener whose policies reflected their needs instead of her own.

My defense policy must seem very erratic – one minute conservative, the next liberal. The aphid invasion this past summer is a perfect example. I was really asleep at the switch when they swarmed over the asparagus bed; in fact they almost destroyed a whole row before I got my act together. Even though two full cans of Raid were stockpiled on the back porch, I went out and bought a new piece of artillery, a container of Rotenone.

I knew the Raid would do the job, but I really don't like the idea of chemical warfare, especially around edible plants. Rotenone is as poisonous as Raid, but only to insects. It's not toxic to humans or domestic animals. It's a resinous substance found in the ground roots of *Derris elliptica,* a tropical leguminous plant. Once extracted, it is mixed into a powder and sometimes combined with a fungicide for the commercial market. It works as a contact insecticide or as a poison affecting a bug's stomach.

In the tropical countries where *D. elliptica* grows, the natives use it to simplify catching fish. The pounded roots are thrown into a stream, temporarily paralyzing the fish. In the garden it can be applied as either a spray or dust. As soon as I sprinkled it on my asparagus, those aphids keeled over, either numb or with such bad stomach aches they could no longer function.

I guess I could count on a few asparagus votes, but I'm afraid some of my other vegetables would like to run me out of office and get a more liberal gardener on the hill. My fiscal policy is not as tight-fisted as it used to be, but I'm still pretty hard-nosed about welfare, believing in the survival of the fittest. If the new carrots can't cope with a little weed competition or the tomato vines can't stand on their own without some sort of prop, I sometimes help and sometimes don't.

It's not that I'm unsympathetic. It's just that quite often I have better things to do. I'm sure my plants would prefer a meticulous sort of gardener, a conscientious candidate who would be consistent in her policies. Growing plants need to know where they stand the same way humans do.

My foreign policy is the only aspect of my reign over Locust Hill's gardens that has been successful, relatively speaking. I haven't vast experience in dealing with foreign vegetables, but I've done well with the few I've planted in the garden. My Chinese edible-pod peas, for instance, peacefully co-exist with other more familiar vegetables in the garden, needing no special attention. The same can be said for my Japanese Daikon radishes.

Have you tried growing these enormous roots? I went out just last week and pulled up three from under the mulch to slice into a salad. They were as big around as a broom handle, not quite as long (about eight inches), pure white and remarkably mild-flavored. They can be sliced into a salad or used with a dip as appetizers. They have a woody taste, however, if they've been cooked.

Well, good or bad, there are no other candidates on Locust Hill offering to take my place in the garden. And there's one thing my vegetables can't complain about – I *never* make promises to them that I don't keep. Now what politician can make that statement?

A DIFFERENT VIEWPOINT

It probably took close to 25 years to turn Locust Hill from a run-down farm into an attractive property. Once we'd really gotten the place in good shape, we considered our little farmhouse, surrounded by rolling meadows and pastures, a small piece of paradise – as close to heaven as we might ever get. The pond shimmered in the sunlight both summer and winter; the lawns and landscape planting were pleasing to the eye. But a few years ago we got a very different viewpoint about this beloved farm that we'd worked and slaved over and delighted in for so many years.

We'd suddenly realized the time had come to start worrying about Uncle Sam getting too big a share of our assets when we kicked the bucket. Land prices had floated higher than a hot-air balloon since we'd bought our 250 acres. If we didn't begin giving it to the kids, they'd be forced to sell some of it to pay the estate taxes.

I find estate planning about as cheerful as going to funerals, but attending to the former and attending the latter are important. Once we'd figured out all those fancy lawyer's phrases – annual gift tax exclusions, fractional shares, tenants in common – we hired an appraiser.

Naturally, for tax purposes, we hoped the appraisal of Locust Hill would be as cheap as its nickname, Low Cost Hill, but we couldn't imagine how that could be managed, knowing that several much smaller properties in the area had recently sold for over a million dollars.

The appraiser, however, was looking at Locust Hill through the eyes of a rich New York house hunter. Potential buyers wealthy enough to consider a 250-acre property are normally not enthusiastic about a small, crooked farmhouse of unpainted clapboards, weather-stained and darkening with age.

This house may have been built in the early 1800s, but it has no beautifully wide floor boards or handsome fireplaces.

What it does have is a dirt (quite often mud) cellar floor and perennial leaks in the roof. Although we like the fact that the dining room has no electricity, forcing us to eat by candlelight every night, I doubt if many people would find this lack of electrical outlets very appealing.

Looking around outside, I realized that to a potential buyer our hilltop acres weren't quite perfect either. There are no magnificent trees, no intricately laid stone walls, no fancy plantings of azaleas or rhododendrons.

Most of the outbuildings sag as badly as they did in 1962. The two sheep pastures, in past years picturesquely clipped by a flock of wooly sheep, had become frowzy with overgrown grass and frost-nipped thistles, since our sheep had been devoured by coyotes the previous year and had yet to be replaced. Who would consider our fake outhouse preferable to the sight of the bulbous propane tank?

We consider our rubber-lined pond more attractive than a swimming pool, but since it collects fallen apples, autumn leaves and plenty of silt each spring, as well as housing frogs, and an occasional turtle, the appraiser wasn't impressed. And as for our rolling meadows, they turned out to be anything but prime farmland. According to the Litchfield County Farm Bureau the soil is of poor quality, and consequently produces poor quality hay. Beyond the meadows there is little but scrub woodland, the decent timber having been cut to help put kids through school.

The fact that the farm sits in luxurious privacy at the end of a dead-end road, something we think of as a major asset, the appraiser viewed as a liability. Just because we consider privacy the ultimate luxury and love living in this isolated spot, doesn't mean others would. Some might find living here scary, other could consider it excruciatingly boring.

I was amazed to find that even Locust Hill Road was, in the appraiser's opinion, a drawback. When I pointed out that it was plowed and maintained by the town right to our front door, he replied in a disparaging voice, "No New

Yorker wants to drive by a house with a dead deer or a goose carcass hanging from a tree, old rusty cars in the yard, falling down chicken coops, piles of old lumber..."

Well, I've been driving up and down our dead-end road for more than thirty years, and none of those things have ever bothered me in the slightest, but if they could help to keep down the value of the Taylor "estate," I say the more the merrier.

We all know that a glass of water can be either half full or half empty, that liberals and conservatives are worlds apart, that some people are born spenders and others born savers, some fanatical athletes and others couch potatoes, but it was quite a revelation to see Locust Hill through the hard eyes of an appraiser.

We still think we live in a little piece of paradise. Such wonderful memories come flooding back as I step out the front door – the sight of over 100 turkeys marching up the road at dawn; the warm camaraderie as our whole family scrambled to get a pile of hay bales into the barn before a thunderstorm; the sight of a mother ewe unexpectedly surrounded by newborn triplets.

Ah, but even Paradise needs constant repair. Last year the old split-rail fence in back of the perennial border began tilting toward the ground, its posts rotting. Obviously the entire fence must soon be replaced. The lower pasture has been taken over by multiflora roses and not even the burro can burrow his way through their thorny branches.

Of course that's really what makes Locust Hill so special – the sweat and tears and memories that have gone into it. Our energy levels are shrinking as fast as our age levels are rising, but the fun of trying to keep our bit of Paradise up to snuff is still with us. Who knows whether our children will feel that way when we're no longer around, but we hope whoever ends up on Locust Hill will have as much fun with it as we've had.

INDEX